Bad Habits

Effective Technique to Break Bad Habits

(Workbook on Building Good Habits & Breaking Free From Bad Habits)

Frederick Karnes

Published By **Phil Dawson**

Frederick Karnes

Bad Habits: Effective Technique to Break Bad Habits (Workbook on Building Good Habits & Breaking Free From Bad Habits)

ISBN 978-1-7776534-1-5

Legal & Disclaimer

Table Of Contents

Chapter 1: What Is The Harmful Behavior?

DRINKING EXCESSIVELY

Everyone knows smokers. Smoking cigarettes is an unhealthy habit due to the negative consequences it can have on your health as well as the impact on relationship with others. If you're part of a smoking group of acquaintances, you may also have non-smokers that will feel offended you decide to smoke with their friends.

A different bad habit is to drink in excess. A drink every occasionally is fine However, drinking too much can cause more harm to your health as well as a loss of relationship or your financial prosperity as (1) drinking is expensive and (2) drinking isn't highly productive when you're drinking or feeling hungover. They can even destroy the four foundations of happiness, health, wealth and joy, just similar to a smashed ball.

Some other bad habits include having a meal out that is greasy or heavy meals frequently, or getting up late or staying up later and also spending excessive time looking at your social media profiles instead of getting to work on something that makes you feel truly content. If people think of undesirable habits, they tend to think of things the body does to them however, there are also negative habits such as saying "Um," and, "Hmm," or even keeping grudges. Socializing with certain individuals can be harmful, when it's detrimental for the rest of your daily life.

You're sure to note down bad behaviors in your daily life. Go to the beginning and start now. Note down 5-10 undesirable habits that you recognize are present within your own life which you've decided to eliminate. It is crucial to be intentional, as it is essential to deliberately and consciously want to be able to rid of them.

Positive reinforcement

I'll tell you a bit about positive reinforcement. Positive reinforcement dates back to many centuries. It's basically our brain's way to say, "Hey, I'm hungry. What can we do?" It perceives food. And the food is consumed which makes you feel happy and your brain is overflowing with dopamine. Dopamine can be a chemical that's produced in the brain every time there is a positive experience for us which is often linked to rewards. The feeling of satisfaction can boost motivation because the brain is saying "Hey, this is awesome, let's do it more often." It also encourages that behavior: it tells you, "Next time we're hungry, how about we eat some food?" The cycle goes continues, and it gets progressively more complicated over the course of your existence. Then, eventually, a habit forms. This positive reinforcement is what can make a habit.

There are times when they can lead to bad behaviors. Similar to smoking cigarettes, a person may begin smoking cigarettes at the age of high school, or even in middle school or college. Due to a myriad of motives (they have a bad feeling, are with their peers and have been pushed to conform and so on) They decide to try smoking. Even though initially it is a pain (anyone who's ever had the pleasure of trying smoking cigarettes knows that it's painful at first and you wheeze, cough then your body warns you that it's not the best). Why do they keep smoking?

As they're influenced by their peers, they begin becoming "cool" and popular, they become rebellious and distinctive that all trigger emotions of dopamine throughout the brain. Naturally smoking cigarettes plays a role too but it's nowhere near as addictive as being accepted and admired by your friends - even when you commit a sin and even if it's better than having no appreciation at all. Dopamine is an emotional boost, and eventually becomes a habit and is extremely difficult to break several years later.

Similar to food. If you're experiencing sadness one day, and you decide to eat a box of ice cream and you are feeling satisfied (sugar is always helpful) What you'll realize is that each time you are feeling sad it's like you're craving the ice cream.

Triggers

You've probably recorded the top 10 behaviors you wish to rid yourself of. The next step to draw the line of a small inch-wide line and identify the items that cause you to fall into the behavior. If you smoke why do you smoke? If you consume Ice cream, what triggers that you to consume Ice cream? It could be because stress is a factor, or you could smoke simply because that's your normal time that you want to, or simply because you're in a group with your buddies.

It is essential to understand triggers as it is difficult to break the bad habit if you are unable to identify the trigger. Each habit is triggered by that occurred when positive reinforcement started. The trigger can be due to the desire to eat, or being with an intimate small group of friends.The trigger might be coming back from work and you find a bottle of alcohol in your refrigerator.

Today, we can employ positive reinforcement to break the cycle of bad habits through removing the trigger. If you remove the alcohol in your refrigerator and then return home, you'll be less likely to consume the alcohol. If you can stop the friends are always smoking around with, perhaps even at that particular time of the day, you can do something different, such as going to the park. Look for the triggers that are causing you to be unhappy within your own life and then try to eliminate them of them.

If your primary trigger for smoking is going out for lunch with a group of acquaintances. Your friends are all smoking cigarettes, they're having lunch, and it's noon. It's time to locate the trigger, and then eliminate the trigger. In essence, you need to destroy the rest of your positive reinforcement. Then it will crumble. When you see food, consume food and you're happy. Friends are around Smoke and you then get more relaxed. If you can get rid of your friends hanging out portion, that totally eliminates all the other aspects of your habits, such as the trigger as well as the reward.

A study was conducted on smokers: researchers sought to discover and study what they could do in order to stop them from smoking. In order to do this, they asked smokers to be mindful. Mindfulness means being present and being aware of the things you're doing. Most people while smoking, are completely unaware. They're not even considering smoking cigarettes, it's merely an habit. It was a bit of mindfulness that helped in removing smoking cigarettes, as people began contemplating what smoking was damaging their bodies. The thing that made it three to 6 times as efficient, was being mindful and interested.

Inquiring about what smoking cigarettes were impacting their body and wanted to find out "What is this really doing to my lungs? What is this doing to my family? What is this doing to make me a better person?" The process of self improvement is vital since you have to possess that mental capacity to be aware of how you're thinking, as well as how you can change your thinking when you are trying to kick an addiction. The final conclusion of the study was that the higher likelihood for them to quit smoking later on in the event that they had an awareness of their actions each time they took of smoking cigarettes was a thought of, "This is filling my lungs with all kinds of negative toxins, and I'm literally taking years off my life statistically."

It helps to be aware, and pose questions to yourself such as "What is this thing that I'm doing? What is this doing to our relationship?" It is important to comprehend the habits you're using, then look at them from a different angle and ask yourself, "Is this profiting me, or is this putting me in the hole in money? Am I losing money, am I lowering the value of my friendships? Am I losing years of my life?"

Ask yourself these questions about the practices on your checklist. It is important to know what this habit does to your body, well-being, your money as well as your relationship with love and even your joy.

Positive punishment

Positive punishment can be thought of as positive reinforcement but instead of receiving a reward you are given a fee or a negative punishment for what you did. As an example, if you begin smoking cigarettes, if you ignite the cigarette, smoke it with your hand then continue smoking for a long time, I'm sure that within 10 to 15 attempts at performing this method, if perform it repeatedly, each time the brain's neural pathways will begin to change it's wiring a in the beginning and you'll be thinking "Oh man, I gotta go back outside and burn myself again?"

It's not my intention to suggest to you that you take this on you, but I'm attempting to assist you in using this concept. It's time to take some form of positive punishment that will make you reevaluate your choices and to think "Oh, instead of maybe just going outside and smoking, maybe I'll go outside and smoke with a person I do not like." When you first start considering smoking and you'll begin to think "Oh how

I'm going to feel the moment lunch arrives, I'll take a trip out to talk with the person. They'll call me out for something I've done wrong." You can keep your stash of cigarettes in an unaccessible location, and each time you get the desire to smoke, you head there to smoke just one smoke. You'll have to work harder each time and until you've lost desire to continue.

I've written many articles about smoking the thing I'd like you to try is regardless of any undesirable habit you possess, change it by reverse engineering it into the smoking examples I've used. Positive reinforcement. Remove of triggers.Positive punishment. You need to consider what you can use to create a trigger whenever you wish to perform an unwelcome action and stop you from doing it from doing the thing and cause you to consider it twice before doing the thing.

Be careful about the punishing yourself in a positive way. If you persist for repeatedly or an incorrect way the term is "Learned helplessness." It's an event where someone commits a crime that is done repeatedly and claim, "I've done it, I've tried it for 10 years, and I can't stop smoking." It's actually a strong mental condition that makes you believe that no matter what you try, nothing is going to change - but that's certainly not the case the case if you're not really looking to take a step towards making a change. However, don't fret that there are millions of people that are suffering from this condition. I'm calling it a disorder because it's an attitude that needs to be dealt with.

Chapter 2: Your Brain Knows That

if it senses an opportunity to trigger what it is used to, it will receive the reward and in time this is all it needs it wants: a reward, and the (if there is a possibility, immediate) instant gratification. In some instances, the brain doesn't even consider the trigger and instead moves to the habit, and then the reward. However, what could we do is to change our habit - that part in between - to one that is more efficient and provides us with the reward. It is possible that we be triggered, such as a break everybody else goes out smoking. Instead of smoking, we could avoid them and take a different route while still getting the dopamine rush. It's still a habit however it's been altered.

The Old Man

It's the story of an elderly man suffering from dementia, and an long history of alcoholism who was in his 70's and 80's with no energy and could barely sit or eat on his alone, but every day shaving his beard was a habit he had cultivated which was a ritual so established during his time in the army and that he was unable to quit regardless of the age or how sick. The man was unable to do anything, but the brain

kept recollecting: "if it's morning, I have to go grab my electric razor and shave my beard". The habit remained due to the fact that habits are formed in the basal Ganglia which is among the most ancient structures of the brain. It's located near the middle of the skull. It's in the area where the spinal cord getting into the brain. This is an extremely older part of the brain. This is the reason the man, even though he got old and had a brain that had been damaged due to disease or drinking, the habit was in the brain because this part of the brain was healthy.

Most individuals, after suffering brain injury, begin losing their memory due to it's located in the prefrontal cortex and on the other parts. However, the area where habits develop is located deep within the brain, and it is difficult to destroy. This is why they are strong and important. You need to be aware of the effects they have on your daily life.

There's a trigger, then there's the habit followed by the rewards. It's time to tackle the middle part (the habit) that is drinking, smoking and the frequent use of social networks, the going to bed in the morning mindlessly but not accomplishing anything worthwhile, sleeping in bed all the time - all of those behaviors that have a root and are destroying your enjoyment in life.

Therefore, you should find something people generally love however is slightly distinct - something that is more positive. In the case of a large number smokers, are able to identify their triggers so instead taking a break at the same time when they normally smoke, they'll try things similar to eating Twizzlers. The smoking of cigarettes has a great deal of psychological issues involving fixation around the mouth since it's related to your breathing in and breath out. It also is a lot in common with the habit of fiddling around on their hands. People like to play with their cigarettes around. In addition, drinkers can be seen drinking people twirling their cups. Additionally, there are other aspects of their psychology. Therefore, it's best to choose an approach that's similar to the routine, but more effective.

Instead of smoking, it is possible to consume Twizzlers Some people take up chewing gum - and it's healthier to chew gum for 24 hours every day rather than smoking 3 hours every day. It is also important to choose an item that can still provide some satisfaction, and that's where the creative aspect is a key element. It's possible to consider about this for a while as it's will lay the groundwork that will allow you to be an extremely successful individual later on.

When you start thinking about this today to make it an everyday habit, it could develop into a concrete plan in the future. Then it won't be necessary to be thinking about this anymore. Instead of rushing out to smoke a cigarette or a cigarette, you can mindlessly chew gum. It's much more enjoyable. One thing you should know about habitual behavior is that most time they can be distracting so they can keep the mind on. This means that you may not be aware of an habit. That's why I would suggest getting out with a few of your acquaintances and say, "Hey listen, be honest with me. I'm trying to become a better person. If there are any habits that have ever offended you, that have affected the quality of our relationship, or even if you think that I should change, tell me now. I need to know." It is important to find an individual who is honest about it, as I know friends who won't talk about things that might be inappropriate to discuss. This can also strengthen to the bond.

How do we transform those bad habits to something new, more beneficial? The trigger is there, such as going outdoors and it could be an unpleasant feeling, such as anxiety or stress, or it could be another thing altogether and you can fill in the blank by naming your motivations to engage in undesirable behaviors. When the trigger occurs then you must be mindful and switch the activity of drinking or smoking or something else. It could be or some other fun and easy option for your needs right now. This could be taking a few deep breaths, sipping the water in a glass and stretching, or doing 10 squats or squats, chewing gum or washing your office.

It's possible that you are spending way too much time browsing your social media accounts, and this is a habit you'd like to rid yourself of. If you ever feel an urge to log on the accounts, consider what the situation may be - perhaps you're with friends but you're not discussing something that is really fascinating. Note that as the reason. This trigger is what makes one want to sign up on Facebook and Instagram and Twitter or whatever other website you'd like to visit to see which one you are accustomed to. It's a habit of getting onto these websites and you get the pleasure of the rush of adrenaline you feel when you see how many people like you've got, or the new comments that you have received and also others' lives and amazing things they perform. If you are aware that your trigger is a boring discussion, instead of constantly using your mobile it is possible to make the conversation more interesting and change the topic or think of suggestions for an activity that you can try. You went out with friends as you love the relationships with them. So, stick to this. There will be lots of time to look up your mobile afterward.

When you're convinced that you require that rush for a negative behavior, you should take a different action that boosts your adrenaline (depending on the situation and the situation) or go for a ride, going out cycling, taking a swim, hiking or even having a chat with the cute woman which makes your heart beat around 160 beats in a minute. Simply something that will get your heart pumping. It's almost distracting.

Then you'll be thinking about it over the next few days, and all sorts of issues, when you're able to break a negative habit, you can look at the issue from a different viewpoint and ask, "How can I get rid of this? Well I can distract myself. Instead of going and drinking when I'm stressed, I can go do something else that pumps me up, gets me excited, motivated. Replace those bad habits with good habits."

Here are three quick tips for ways to transform bad habits to good ones as well as help to create more successful healthier habits.

1. Find individuals who share similar lifestyles. As an example, one major reason that a large number smokers smoke is because many of their acquaintances smoke. the pressure from peers means that you're your own five people are the ones you spend your most time with. If you're always with people who smoke and drinking, the habit will begin be instilled into you. If you're in a group of those who do not smoke or drink, who aren't drinking, you're with people who take to skydiving on a regular basis, there are people around you who wish to create a successful business which is what you'd like to pursue, or if you're hosting the best photography show ever, and you're looking to accomplish then you're the one to be hanging out with. If you're looking to break free of your negative habits, begin being around people that would ridicule you over this habit, and tell you, "Hey you need to change that if you

want to hang around with us." It should be a motivator for you.

2. Eliminate triggers as well as any other thing that you are able to imagine could lead to an eventual habit of bad behavior. It is essential to discover the triggers, and you must be aware of what is causing these triggers, and then you have remove these triggers.

3. Change your environment. Sometimes, people need an adjustment in their thinking to open their minds. to become more open. And often to achieve this, you need to modify the environment around you. Have you been at a beach and you get an thought? Sometimes, you'll get these wild concepts simply because you're not part of the environment. And your thinking "Look at all this new data, look at all this new information, look at ... What can we do with that?" Your brain is able to think of innovative ways of solving issues

and will come up with innovative solutions. So just entering a different environment in a new place, with people who are different from you, and around fresh experiences will aid in breaking out of bad habits faster.

What is the time frame?

There are many individuals who think it will be 21 days for the creation of an habit. It could take up to up to 67 days for the formation of the habit. The main reason why they believe that it is due to the fact that although the motivation for you will fade during those times however, you maintain the habit and discipline. You've got a routine to continue doing it. People who start January 1st and who are just beginning to go to the gym say they need to do it for 21 or 67 times for forming a habit as it is usually much lower than this. The thing they would like that you do is keep going until you become disciplined.

They do this since they want you to realize that you'll be required to stay longer than you think is necessary to ensure you can be disciplined.

It's a simple technique that can help you establish an immediate habit change or transform an old one into a positive one. It's getting your brain to open and recognizing that your habit is evolving today and it's happening right now. It's important to do this when your mindset change to "I got to do this 21 days so the habit will change" That is, it's going take the required 21 to 21 days. If you think that your habit is going to alter today, then you can expect it to change now since your mind is the aid in changing and you'll begin to develop the habit immediately. Naturally, it's important to repeat the process. The trick is to practice things repeatedly for a long time. For certain people, it may take 21 days posting daily video to your YouTube channel until your channel is booming. Others you could need up to 67 videos. The trick is to persist until you are able to maintain your routine down and it will become simpler and easier to follow it.

What I found to work for me as I began the YouTube channel I had thinking it was "You know what? Right now, right this second I'm going to work and persevere and keep going until this channel is successful." This wasn't an habit. It was not like "I'm going to do this habit now and then tomorrow I'm going to do the same habit, and then the day after that I'm going to do the same habit, for 21 days hoping that it will last" This wasn't as if I had manipulated myself to be disciplined. This was the moment that I said "today, I'm going to make a change. I'm going to impact people's lives. I'm going to work and continue making great videos forever". This isn't considered a decision to live by.

Make sure you don't "program" your mind with the length of time. In the case of some diets, they'll say "for thirty days, I'm going on this diet, and shed some pounds, then go back to having a normal diet "normally" and maybe I'll gain some back". The truth is that they do gain the weight back because they aren't able to develop that discipline. The mind of the person is set for the 30-day period to change their eating patterns, and at the conclusion of their 30 day period, they simply return to the old routines. If you declare, "I'm going to do it for 67 days" You may have started an habit but eventually, you'll fall off the track.

The key is to recognize that if you wish to establish a habit, you must say "This habit is going to be there for the rest of my life," not just for 21 consecutive days or the 67 days. The process is beginning now, and it's running until I'm dead. It's a habit that will stay with me forever.

From now on, every day I'm planning to rise to run 6 miles. The goal is not "until I have great abs" since then you'll have abs, and the routine is going to begin to disappear and you'll not possess abs at all anymore. This isn't "until I lose 60 pounds" because after you've lost 60 pounds, it will be difficult to maintain it anymore. Then you'll gain those 60 pounds back.

Every day from to now, I'm you're thinking "I'm going to use this habit to make me better". "Every week I'm going to post at least three videos". "Every day I'm going to go on a six mile bike ride". "Every day instead of smoking I'm going to eat six Twizzlers". "Every day I'm going to find one person to hang around who will make me a better person". "Every day I'm going to talk to at least one girl so that my social anxiety is reduced". This is not "every day I'm going to talk to a girl until my social anxiety is gone" however "every day until I die I'm going to talk to a girl because I want that continual improvement". There won't be a final objective. There will be objectives however there will not have a goal at the end because it is always improving.

The same is true for you. You should be planning how you will complete your work. There's no way to do it in 21 days after which it becomes effortless. It will get simpler and more simple eventually, until maybe sixty years from now, there's no need to consider the idea. You just have to say, "Oh, I didn't do those 50 push-ups today and my muscles are asking for it. Oh, I haven't went for a bike ride today. I need to go do that. Oh, I haven't done my budget this month. I also need to do that."

Do not believe the 21 day routine myth. Get rid of the 67 myth about habit and begin thinking about the instant that you're starting the habit of today just now beginning today, and going for the rest of your life, which is why it's immediately and for ever. Start your new habits today. You shouldn't claim that you'll start next week. "Tomorrow" is like a beautiful day where wonderful things will happen, but it's not real. There is always today. You shouldn't claim that you'll start within a week. Set them up immediately and permanently and not just until you reach your goal. and not until you've lost at least 60 pounds. Not until you've got an unbeatable six-pack and never stop for a while.

There are many objectives. For instance, you could declare "when I get a six pack then I can eat half a tub of ice cream or when I get a six pack then I'll go on a cruise". Keep those practices for a long time as if they're never going to last forever and you're not planning to maintain them forever it's not actually practices. The same goes for diets. If you achieve your goal then the routine will fall out of your life and after that you'll increase your weight by 60 pounds.

In the next section, we'll discover how you can make new habits that are great from scratch by understanding the trigger-habit reward concept of a habit as well as some additional strategies you could employ for putting that habit into place. The key is to recognize that once you create routines, they are immediately and keep them for the rest of your life.

Chapter 3: In The Past, We've Focused On The Process Of Identifying

Bad habits and then getting rid of the bad habits Also, we've discussed the replacement of bad habits by healthy habits. In this segment, we're going explore trigger-based reward development as well as how you can develop your own habits.

It is possible to incorporate this into all aspects of your daily life. If you're trying to stay healthier, that could mean running or a bike ride, and eating healthier meals. For the aspect of wealth it is possible to consider making investments in higher education as well as having better managing your finances in your personal family. There is always more to learn about everything as learning is the best way to increase the amount of money you have in the form of love and joy.

Additionally, you can improve your behavior regarding happiness and love by gaining more knowledge on the areas of study. The concept of love is different since there are lots instances when you just don't desire to experience the feeling. If you want to appreciate someone else, however it is also possible to implement many small habits to make the person feel valued. Let's look at the reward of trigger habit.

You should take a piece paper. Then, in the center of the page, write down 5-10 ways you would like to develop. On the left, you'll put your triggers. In my case, for instance, on my piece of paper, I'm planning to place the words "reading. I'm planning to read for at least 30 minutes every day, which is the central point of my sheet of paper. This will be my habit column. On the left there will be The trigger column.

In order for me to be motivated to go to the library, I'm going need to think of an event that occurs throughout the day to say "Hey, this trigger is fulfilled. Let's go on to the habit." My trigger, located on the other aspect of reading will be getting up. When I get up I do the very initial thing that I'll do prior to then I'm the reading. As time it will turn into routine.

Another column to fill in which is the one where you will find the reward. If you have the trigger on the left side, your habit is in the middle and the reward on the right. My trigger is getting up. My habit is to read, and the reward will be breakfast.

There are a variety of advantages available. The choice is entirely up to you the things you think are satisfying. Breakfast is a pleasure to me, especially after having spent eight hours in bed. I get up after which I read before having breakfast. In time the process will establish a pattern to the point where when I do not read, I'm almost ashamed of being up at 5am and having breakfast. I'm almost ashamed of having to break that habit, similar to many others who find themselves feeling guiltily guilty whenever they break the bad habits.

Make a list of this, then do it for each routine, no matter if it's studying or taking part in an easy run of one mile. Personally, I prefer running around a mile of running, twice on my street. Running is a routine. It starts with breakfast when I've finished eating my breakfast, I get into the habit phase that I run. Be aware that when you decide to run following a meal, it is best to take a lighter meal to ensure you don't put your body through overly. You should also allow time to digest before you run make sure you don't leap from the breakfast buffet into your sneakers for running and walk go out.

With the habit of running, I can have the habit as well as the pleasure of it all in one step since my one mile of running is so relaxing it doesn't require me to do something else to reward myself in exchange.

Keep in mind that the definition of reward could be any thing you like and have fun with, but it needs to match the thing that you and your brain consider to be enjoyment. It doesn't require eating an entire piece of candy or earn a little cash to be fulfilled. In addition, I enjoy having a shower. I like being clean, particularly in the early hours of the day. I can guarantee that if I can get my nice shower into my bathroom and have completed my exercise and done my short run, I'll feel happier at myself.

Then I go for a shower and I feel great afterwards It's one of the most satisfying experiences ever. I was sweating, I felt pumped as my heart beat and taking that bath felt very calming, If you'd like get it, take one of those cold showers. This is an incredible reward. As you might have noticed, your behaviors are interconnected, each one triggering the next. This can continue like that for the entire day.

This technique actually was sown into Arnold Schwarzenegger when he was young. Prior to eating and eat, he would perform many push-ups. The parents even made him exercise a bit prior to eating - thus his exercise was a routine.

It is possible to make it a routine making contact with your grandmother at least every day when you wish to. You can say, "I'm so thankful you're in my life. I just wanted to appreciate everything you do for me." Anything can be turned into a habit and it doesn't have to be every day. It is possible to turn triggers into routine things. The phone's incline can be an opportunity to phone your grandma to say, "Hey, I just paid my phone bill. I'm so thankful you're in my life," -- is a good idea to make that call every now and then in case you may not have that occasion again.

In the end, it's possible to transform anything into a trigger. You just need to come up with a new idea and allow your brain to associate diverse tasks with various times in the day, or perhaps specific actions you take. There may be one event which happens every year that you wish to transform into trigger. "It's time to pay my taxes, let's go get my dogs their shots so that they're legal in my town". This is a nice method to establish a routine, or you can even make rewards.

Be aware that the more long the time period is, the more difficult it will be to develop a routine, because there are fewer iterations. If something is something you regularly do is more likely to remain with you for a longer time. For instance, if your motivation is watching someone else walk through the aisle and you are prone to making them feel special because you're looking to become better at giving compliments. It is possible that you want to become better at complimenting them, without becoming awkward. Then the reward will be to put the Skittle inside your mouth.

When a person walks past your desk between 6 and fifty times per day in an office that is large it's 50 praises. This is 50 rewards. do you know what else it is? It's a total of 50 times you've done that practice. You can be almost certain that once you've practiced it for a few days, it'll develop into a habit, and you'll never be required to buy yourself the Skittle. If someone passes in front of you, you'll tell them "Hey, Jim. Nice shoes. Love those things." "Hey, Linda. That's a neat shirt." "Hey, John, I noticed you got your hair cut." The hair will grow naturally with time.

It's important to keep your document with triggers to the left with habits at the center and the reward points in the center. Since then, any time you're looking to establish a routine, whether that's giving someone a reward for something they've done, or making an YouTube video, note the details down and store your record in a place where you will quickly see and recall the details. When I publish YouTube videos, I've created a small reward system that I use for myself. When I click"publish" or the "publish" button is like being flooded with dopamine inside my brain because I love hitting that button.

When I'm making the video, the motivation for me is "Oh, man. I'm not getting very many views today." It's the habitual process of creating videos, and it's very difficult and not a lot of fun however I am happy with the result, as well. I enjoy clicking that button to see that there were 600 viewers who saw my video the one second that I uploaded it It's an amazing reward.

The similar thing to making your own YouTube video, to filing your taxes, to obtaining your dog's shots, to whatever behaviors you wish to develop.

One of the most effective ways to create habits, similar to one of the easiest methods to break the habit is simply to swap them because the habit exists already. There's already a trigger and the reward. Now you've need to swap that thing at the middle. It's a lot more challenging to kick the bad habit and it's much more difficult to start an entirely new habit. The easiest way to do this could be to just switch out the middle portion and switch it from smoking cigarettes to reading. Switch it to drinking instead of chewing gum.

There are two other things that can aid you in habit development:

1. Affirmations. The affirmation is something you make yourself believe, which you eventually begin believing and subconsciously begin to act according to the affirmation. Your brain will eventually accept the information as reality - it's a biological response to a mental affirmation. Then you'll be able to say

"Hey, I'm going to go for a run today." This is an affirmation. "Hey, I'm going to be super successful today in my journey of talking to women," in the event that it's an habit you'd like to build and become better in. The best affirmations will be those that are positive. It is always more effective to say, "I will eat healthy food," rather than "I will not eat junk food," due to the fact that the brain is unable to process negative thoughts. If I ask you to not think of a yellow squirrel, what's the first thought that comes to mind? It's a yellow squirrel. If you believe that eating more healthy food, imagine the food you'll crave eating all of the junk food that's available particularly due to being a "forbidden" aspect (that you chose to reduce your intake of it). Therefore, the affirmations must be positive. It is important to focus focused on the things you'll do rather than things you don't perform.

2. If-Then Statements. When you consider an habit, you'll require at least some discipline when you create it, as you'll need to recognize that this will not happen overnight, except if you are forced to think instantly and for a long time (see the preceding chapter).If you are having trouble in this regard, think of an If-then statements: "If I create this habit of going for a walk every each day, and I begin making a list of my meals every day that I'll be healthier, that is, I'll have the six-pack. And then I'll get better at interacting with women. In turn, my financial situation will improve".

If-then phrases are small stimulants. In addition to affirmations, they can be extremely efficient in the formation of routines.

Chapter 4: It Is Important To Recognize

The fact that by incorporating these principles to your lifestyle it is not going to make you immediately success However, looking at successful individuals and attempting to emulate their methods within our lives increases our odds of becoming successful just like them. Here's what they're doing:

1.CREATING A TO DO LIST

1. Creating a to-do list.

The most successful people create a daily to-do checklist in the morning. They are crucial because when you don't set the goal of the things you'll complete that day, then you'll go about your day feeling lost. It's unlikely that you'll complete all the tasks you could actually complete by writing your list of things to do. It's important to remember that when you write a list of tasks, you should write concrete tasks. Therefore, you shouldn't write "I am going to work on a website." This is just too vague, and could cause you to feel unmotivated and could be tempted to delay your efforts since you aren't sure where to start. You should instead note down specific actions such as "implement a new page and write 1000 words of content" and "mow the lawn by 3:00."

2. Energizing

If successful people get up and get up, they take action to get their energy back. It can be as simple as taking a walk or doing a exercise, or stretching to 10 mins. If you're not feeling like getting up and moving then you can drink your coffee or have a hot shower. When you enter the bathroom and switch on the shower the water will hit your body and make you breathe deeply. The blood will begin flowing through all the organs in your body and this is an excellent method to get you going.

3. Scheduling

In addition to having your list of tasks but you must also keep a calendar of the time that you'll accomplish certain items on the to-do list. For instance, you may need to trim the lawn, or you may need to make a video and then you'll need to prepare your dinner. It's possible to get all of the tasks done in three hours which will feel good as you cross each of them off. Another thing that is great what successful people do which they make into a daily routine is to tell yourself "I will cut the lawn by 10 in the morning. I will create a YouTube by one in the afternoon. And I will fix dinner by six tonight." This will give you security knowing you've set a time to do that task only. It helps to avoid putting off work throughout the day only to be in a panic when you realize and realize that you've never completed a task on your list of things to do.

4. Early risers

There's plenty of people who are truly prosperous, and who sleep up until 11:30 at the end of the day. What I've observed is that there are a number of individuals who aren't only highly successful but also very successful, such as Sam Walton, who build massive businesses, those who are like Arnold Schwarzenegger, and people such as Aaron of Alpha M. is that they rise early (I am referring to early or early). Many people get up around six, and that's an early start. If you wake up around five, it gives an additional time to outdo the clock. You'll have an additional period of time in which for more work. Also, it is important to take a good amount of sleep to ensure you're getting adequate rest also. It is possible to take an afternoon nap or get up an hour earlier at night as your brain gets exhausted and unable to function regardless.

5. The power of affirmations and visualization

Two completely distinct items, however I've put them together because they complement each other really well. Affirmations are similar to affirming yourself about what you're planning to accomplish today: "I will become successful. I will do the dishes. I will make 50 dollars today by selling a product. I will finish the last 60 pages of this book" These are affirmations. These are affirmations. A different aspect is visualizing the events that you're looking for. It is possible to imagine what the website will look after it is completed, and how beautiful your kitchen will look after all the dishes are cleaned and all the kitchen appliances in place. The outcome you can visualize from your efforts and work acts as a powerful incentive. When you're able to think about these things and visualize them, it can help you lay the foundations to move across them and reach your destination.

6. Gratefulness

Feeling grateful for something at the beginning of your day when you first get up is awe-inspiring as there's a lot of benefits out of it. This sets you in a positive direction to start your day. Right from beginning to end, you'll have the feeling of happiness and it is reflected in every thing you do during the day. It's a little difficult when you wake up and think "I'm so grateful I get to take a cold shower." However, I'm sure you could be thankful for all sorts of other things such as seeing clearly or even all of your fingers. If you don't possess 10 fingers, then you may be blessed with eight fingers - but it's still a blessing for having eight fingers. You can accomplish many things using your fingers. There's plenty to be thankful for. All you have to do is put your mind in a grateful situation because this will prompt your brain to feel happy which will eventually turn into a routine and, over time your success will become more apparent to the person you are. When others see you, and are able to think positively and positivity, they'll want to be alongside you, take time with you, and assist to support you in a variety of ways. It is possible to see gratitude as the base of your day. If you're grateful at the beginning of your day, and you're likely have an amazing day. It's going require a significant amount of effort to transform an awful day into one that starts by waking up thinking "Man, I'm so glad I get to stand up. I'm glad I got toes on my feet, and I can see clearly. It's just amazing. Even if I can't see clearly, I'm glad someone invented glasses and contacts that I can put in my eyes and still see clearly."

7. A bonding moment with a person early on

The human bond is an extremely essential thing. It's especially important when you're living with one another. If you're sharing a home with someone else, one of the first things you do in the morning ought to be showing the love they deserve. It could involve hugging them by making them coffee or cuddling. This releases lots of Oxytocin (a hormone which is linked directly to human bonds, increasing the trust and commitment) in the early hours in the morning, it makes you feel good. It's like saying "Wow, I love this person. I love being around this person. I'm so glad this person is in my life." If you can do this it's an excellent routine to develop as you develop the relationship. You build trust, and the relationship likely to develop in time. This is something you need to keep working at every single day.

8. Clean up after the night's sleep.

If you're anything like me, there's a chance you've gotten lots of work to do in the past, particularly as an business owner. There are many employees in the office who don't necessarily require this advice, however If you're an entrepreneur who is building a company or you were up at night ...your workspace could be full of pile of clutter (and even when you weren't up all night, it's not uncommon that this takes place). It's much easier to get it cleaned up to clean up the mess early in the day. This is because that usually, later in the day your decision-making processes are not your best. When you wake up in the morning, when you're fresh and eager to begin the day, it's easy to think "All right, now I have the discipline and willpower built up in me because I got enough sleep that I can clean my desk." It's a lot more challenging to accomplish that task after a working day in the event that you're tired and all you're thinking about is going to sleep.

9. Silence

It is essential to be quiet, particularly when you're an introvert as introverts are recharged by the silence. For instance, I like getting up at 6 am to drink a cup of coffee, and enjoying the time of my life in the morning when no one else is awake. When that cup of coffee just begins to enter my system It's an instant of pure bliss. And I'm able to feel clear and can see what my goal is throughout the day. This is the way I can get an enormous amount of work accomplished. It's possible that anyone can benefit also from this. This might not work as effectively for extroverts as their brains require more stimulation to be happy and feel good, however it will definitely help introverts. Morning silence can help you focus your mind and help you know what you need to accomplish throughout the day.

10. Then, I read about the events of in the evening prior

This can benefit lots of people when they incorporate it as a routine for their mornings. It is possible that there were events that occurred while you were sleeping things could be happening in another country, or things could have occurred in the workplace if it's an ongoing work. Be aware that you're probably trying to avoid items that aren't important or negative. A lot of suburban stories about "24 people killed that night." It's vital, but you don't have to use it in order to reach the goals you set as it could impact your performance negatively. It's also trivial for instance, a person might have been crowned a winner of a spelling competition. There's no need to search the media to find out that. It's not necessary to find out that you're sleeping due to someone winning the spelling competition, except for your best friend or child isn't likely to help you when it comes to your accomplishments.

The 10 best daily habits of people who are successful. If you have a few of these in your daily routine If so, great! It's a good thing. If you're not using them, try the strategies and find out what will work best for your needs. We will then look at the twelve habits millionaires possess.

Chapter 5: Everybody Wants To Be Millionaires

If that's the case too, then you may like to look at the lifestyles of millionaires and then what they have done so successfully that has helped them achieve the success they have achieved? Sure, understanding the right habits and applying them won't guarantee quick success However, they could aid you towards realizing your dreams. We'll look into these:

1 HAVING A BUDGET

1. Budgeting is essential.

It could be a monthly budget or a daily budget however, they keep track of their networks based on the income and expenditure. It's something that's bound become a routine when you're trying to incorporate this into your routine. It was something I began at the age of two, and have seen significant change. The first step is to understand the whereabouts of your money as you become cognizant of the money you spend. It's fun to watch the value of your assets increase.

2. Being proactive

Being proactive implies taking charge to your actions and life in order to make things happen rather than sitting and waiting for them to be thrown into the air. It is rare for miracles to occur, and if you wish to lead a fulfilled prosperous, fulfilled life, then you need to do your part to achieve that. Therefore, you must be prepared before things happen by addressing all the small aspects of your work prior to getting the feedback of the boss or your customer. Do not wait around for them to inform you how to proceed, be prepared and think ahead, doing your best to do top-quality work. It will surely get noticed, and you could end getting more commission requests as well as growing your business. This is true for all aspects of your daily life. As an example, clean the dishes prior to them get until the ceiling is reached you can ask a person to go out on a date as opposed to checking your mobile every day to find out whether they've invited you.

3. Reading

I can't stress enough how important this is. I've read a lot of books about success, psychology business as well as self development. A common thread I've noticed among all millionaires is that they've read number of books. They are prone to filling their minds with thoughts, since ideas can be seeds for business, and companies make money. If you'd like to improve the chances of becoming a millionaire, you must study more. Explore more non-fiction, take in more information that can make you more of a individual. Business development and personal development, practically anything you could find begin reading even newspapers. Fill your mind with a variety of thoughts, and the thoughts will soon multiply.

4. Curiosity

This is a connection with reading. If you're reading about something isn't something you're interested in isn't going to be enjoyable. Millionaires are always curious. they are never bored of exploring new ideas, acquiring new talents or testing different methods to improve their job. The key is curiosity. development and development.

5. Explore the fascination

This is a connection to tip four. If you are curious, it is possible to pose a question to yourself however, you need to be willing to hunt for answers. People often pose questions for the purpose of asking questions, or to be smart or to provoke others However, only a few actually explore for answer. Millionaires are those who do not just ask questions however, they also seek solutions.

6. Look for someone to mentor you

Mentors can steer over all sorts of mistakes you could make by yourself if you pay attention to him. There are a lot of people who have made from their mistakes on their own. If you're able to avoid that step, and take lessons from the mistakes of others as they're a mentor for you, it will help you get a head start on becoming millionaires.

7. Goals

The importance of goals is to any part of our lives in the sense that they provide you with motivation as well as assist you in achieving discipline. Making goals, and then reaching the goals you set is extremely rewarding. As an example, I enjoy to compete. I like having greater number of subscribers than others or to produce the most videos than anyone else is an incentive for me. The goals you set must coincide with the things that motivate you. The goal shouldn't be far off in the world, however they should not be too short-sighted. The best advice I can give you is to create objectives that are SMART and that's an acronym which is for Specific, Measurable and Achievable relevant, Achievable, Time-bound. If you make use of all these elements and build an objective that is based on them, it will inspire you to achieve it.

8. Daily list

Each morning, when I get up, I take note of the three things I would like to complete this day. This is extremely important because each time I accomplish something and I complete it and it inspires me to complete another one. If I'm lying on my bed in the evening and something aren't done, I'll get awake at 11:15 at night and tell myself "Hey, I need to get this done. It's making me mad, I can't go to sleep." and I'll do it. It's a motivator for me and I believe it's going to encourage you to do the same. That's what I've discovered quite a bit while studying the lives of a lot of millionaires. They are fond of making lists and arrange their lists as well as use the lists to accomplish their objectives.

9. Are you able to earn multiple income streams?

Being able to have multiple sources of income can feel like a rain of money, and it's a wonderful feeling. This gives you the feeling of peace knowing that regardless what happens to any of your positions or customers, you're secure and can continue to pay your rent or charges. If, for instance, you're an artist and aren't simply relying on a new job to make ends meet, you can also get profits from any work that you've made previously - in essence, this is money that comes to you on an ongoing schedule and which you could make use of for all your essential requirements. Anything that is over that considered a reward that you can utilize to spend time with family, for holidays or for gifts.

10. Not diversify

AKA Focus. There's a good chance you've heard, "Diversify your portfolio and you'll get rich." However, there's a caveat that a majority of millionaires do not make the effort to diversify their portfolios until they're millionaires. In order to become millionaires you put all your eggs in one basket and then make sure to ensure that they don't break any eggs. In the beginning, it is important to concentrate on one area, then get really proficient at this, then only when you are good at it you are able to concentrate on something else. When you think of Mark Cuban, he started an organization, earned an enormous amount of money. Then, later did he start another business, and the focus was on to grow it. He made a amount of money from this one too and keeps doing it. It's a good idea to diversify your business across time as long as you've got an established company or a ability that has earned an excellent reputation and stream of income. If you attempt to concentrate on multiple areas at the same time and you don't have the capacity to devote enough energy into each of them and you'll end up confusing the clients as well. First, they must be aware of the name of your company (or business) first when they first hear about you. Once you're well-known, you're able to expand expanding your offerings.

11. Do not be time waste

There are many things to do in the world, and time which you could be doing that are essentially wasting your time. A common trait of millionaires is to recognize the value and worth to their time. You will never be able to get your time back. When you realize the value of your time, you'll start taking note of the value of your time more. If you are able to appreciate your time and more you'll find that it's easy to stay clear of many time waste. Take for instance, in your Facebook every 30 minutes during the every day. Imagine the amount more efficient you can become if you utilized the time to concentrate to work on your development or write a book. If you spend thirty minutes writing a book over the course of a calendar year, it could be at least two or three published books and I'm almost certain of you'll be able to write. Knowing the worth of your time forces you to reconsider everything that takes away the time of your day. Then you will be able to cut out those things that waste your time and do not provide any benefit.

12. Make sure you focus on the most lucrative actions

Instead of dwelling on insignificant issues or items can drain your bank balance Instead, concentrate on the items that will help you reach that final goal. There is no way to be a millionaire if your only activity using your cash is keep it in a savings account.

Chapter 6: They Are Examples Of Things You Can Emulate Yourself

There are certain things that all people who have successful relationships share and you are able to look and say, "Wow, if I do that, I will have a higher likelihood of having a successful relationship." The word "relationship" can be anything that includes boyfriend, love and girlfriend to marriage up to your close colleagues, friends and even your neighbors. It's a wide range of what it means. This is just a matter of having a wonderful connection.

1. COMMUNICATION

1 Communication

Most difficulties are due to individuals aren't able to convey their emotions and think or what's causing the issue. If you are able to communicate well, it's the base of a good relation. A lot of conflicts arise from a an inability to communicate, due to the fact that different people use different methods of communicating the same thought or idea however, each person is able to interpret it in a specific way, based on the personal experience of each.

Being honest and describing the other person exactly the things you know about something or other thing you heard, may result in a reaction such as "oh I don't know the way I was referring to it. Let me explain how things seem to me". We often get enticed on certain phrases or words and then take them off-hand, and then be angry as it causes us question the concept of what the other person was trying to convey. Speaking up about these issues could help to ease and even eliminate many of the conflicts which may arise in relationships.

2. Forgiveness

It's something you can all find throughout their lives. There are a lot of people who have difficulty in allowing forgiveness to people. A good way to gauge your relationships is to commit an error on purpose, and ask for forgiveness. How they respond can tell the level of trust in the relationship. However, I wouldn't suggest it as long as you don't have a clue. It is possible to do the same for yourself too: Let other people forgive what they've done to them and you'll avoid numerous problems. In the event that you've made an error unintentionally, when you request forgiveness, be sure that you're genuine and truly feel inside that you won't repeat the mistake rather than apology from the corner of your tongue like it's an obligation.

3. Understanding

When you know the person and what they are feeling It becomes much easier to accept their feelings. To truly understand people, you must (at at the very least) place yourself into their shoes and look at the world from their point of view. It is essential to be able for this by developing the empathy part of yourself will improve the effectiveness of your relationships in time. Many conflicts occur as a result of the two (or more) individuals are unable to comprehend each other's viewpoint They may both have the right idea, however their inability to look at things from different perspectives can make things extremely difficult.

It requires a huge heart and an open mind to be able to comprehend someone else's feelings and their life, be able to understand how another person feels however, it can help greatly in bonding with the person. Over time knowing them better can help them to open up to your feelings.

4. Know the five love languages.

If you've been through the book The Five Love Languages, you'll realize the importance of loving someone isn't something you are able to perform passively. The relationship needs to be maintained constantly. You constantly have to work at improving your relationship constantly. time and you shouldn't relax and hope that the relationship will continue to grow as it did it did in the beginning. It is possible to earn an income that is passive into your account without having to think about it. But the way that relationships work isn't always this easy.

In order to ensure that your partner feels accepted by you, you have know what can make them feel valued all over the world. It is common for us to display our appreciation and love for the person we love in a manner that we want to be treated. being aware of our differences can aid us in feeling more connected with our partner.

The five languages comprise affirmations (praise) and services. They also include gifts, high-quality time and physical contact. Everyone's different. It's possible that you'll have a mixture of all these or just one or more of them could be extremely significant for you. If, for instance, I feel appreciated when I am given money or presents and gifts, I might give them to my spouse or partner - since it's the way I express my personal language of affection. If all they require to do is the use of my time and I'm always making money (to generate money to buy them presents) the person aren't feeling loved, in fact, they'll be feeling rejected and unappreciated. Learning the five language of love can assist you to connect with your spouse and make you feel valued and loved when you're in a relationship over longer term. It's all about understanding your own personality and to get to know who you're in with, and your relationships, and the ones you've created in your life. Once you've begun analysing them and discovering the language they use to express love or their top priorities and then you'll be building a more positive relationship regards to how you develop your behavior. Go read the book, because it's worth the effort.

5. Respect

This is essential when it comes to relationships of any type. Look for the good qualities in every person you meet and treat them how you'd want to be treated. Although their work isn't as good as yours, it doesn't necessarily mean they don't deserve more respect. You are more respected than they do. Respect is the basis of harmonious relationships. There are times when you may not be able to like everything someone does or make a few mistakes however it doesn't mean that at any time, you have the right to curse the person, scream at them or make them feel like they're worthless. Be sure to offer your comments with a respectful and calm manner, and look for ways to improve or (if it's even possible) just end the relationship.

6. Recognize each other and show appreciation

It can be as simple as going far back those five languages of love that express gratitude, "I appreciate you. Let's spend 30 minutes together watching the sunset," or "I appreciate you, I wrote you a little note when I thought of you" or "Here's a small gift when I was on vacation." Giving your gratitude through tiny gestures and it's even saying to someone "Hey, I appreciate that you're in my life" This can be very helpful. It helps someone feel appreciated and appreciated, which will make them more likely to show kindness and initiative.

7. The focus should be on the issue at hand and not on the issue at hand.

Often, when the issue arises, people tend to blame one another instead of looking for solutions. If a situation arises, or an error has been made, the primary focus is on solving the issue, instead of putting a burden to the relationship. It doesn't matter who's fault it is, everybody should consider ways to solve the issue before deciding what can be done to prevent such situations to come up in the future. Remember, that there's no "me versus you". Instead, it's "us versus the problem".

Fighting, hurting one another with snide remarks and demeaning each other is not going to help anyone. In fact being hurt, you're unable to think rationally and your motivation to tackle the problem decreases dramatically. Thus, coming together with the words, "You know what? It's not your fault. It's not my fault. It's both of our faults. What can we do to solve this problem?" It will help solve many issues in relationships. This is about working as a unit, no matter it's a marriage group or an a couple team or you even with your acquaintance. If you start thinking about problems and arguing over something that you are able to solve and bond over, you'll be able to strengthen your bond and be more successful with your relationship.

8. Honesty is the first priority

There are a number of occasions in your life you look back on and be thinking,

"Man, it was really easy to lie there," however, in the end, when it comes to the matter, friendships and good relationships are meant to last the long-term. Therefore, if you're looking for an immediate relationship sure, you could do what you want and be honest. However, if you're upfront and honest, not going through many holes, the person you are with will begin to trust your character even more. They'll also be able to understand your personality better, and you'll be able to communicate better with them. Another great fundamental characteristic of a good relationship is to start by being honest with them first. If you're not confident in speaking your truth with someone, it may be some sort of psychological abuse or other issue which is making the relationship difficult to maintain and you'll need to leave this in the end.

9. Take time for one another

It's something that I personally am struggling with, and I believe that a lot of entrepreneurs struggle with this particularly in relational relationships because they are a lot of work. Being a working-holic can be detrimental to the other aspects of your life, particularly in your relationship. When you're having a night out with your significant other and you're not having a wonderful time and you're being thinking "I could be making $5,000 or $10,000 more dollars a month if I spent that time on the business" Instead, think "You are aware that this relationship is the best thing that I have in my life. If I did not enjoy it, I may be unable to commit so hard." This is something must be balanced and it's important to remain mindful of the portion of your life you'd like to spend working as well as what percentage of your daily life you wish to have in your daily life. There's no way you can live living with a billion dollars in a bank account on your own because you've neglected the relationships you have with others for the sake of building that bank.

10. Laugh a lot

There are many benefits for your brain when you laugh frequently. The most common is that you are spending time with someone who's charming, but it's not you that has transformed, it's them, those you're with. They help people feel more attractive and give you the impression that you can laugh and you're allowed to be who you are. If you're able be around people who are similar to them, it's another good habit you can develop to build a strong connection.

Chapter 7: Do You Really Want To Be Content?

Many times, we take actions believing that they'll be a good thing - and this is like putting off our happiness until we have an enormous bank account, or until we meet our perfect match, till... (fill the blank). the in the blank). However, happiness is often found in tiny amounts, and is derived from the smallest every day objects. Therefore, let's take a look at the habits can be incorporated into our lives in order to be happier:

1.GRATEFULNESS

1. Gratefulness

When you get up and be genuinely happy over something, you're more content. Did you wake up with the thought "Today's going to be a bad day. Bad things are going to happen. I'm not going to enjoy doing this task and that task and I have to hang around these people"? You're probably making your life dark and bleak. What it do to your mental state and makes you angry and cranky, which does affect your mood all through the day. In addition, those who are angry will be less likely to get received with respect, as they often behave as mirrors. When you see someone smiling and we smile at them. However, if you see someone smirk and look down, they're in fact darkening the day as we also frown. If you're beginning your day by thinking "I may have some challenges in this particular day of my life, but I certainly have the resources to deal with that, so let's see what I can do to overcome them." This is already making you more efficient and focused in solving issues instead of thinking about "how bad it's going to be". When you start the day with gratitude and positive thoughts, you're making your mind come up with ways to make you more content.

2. Optimism

It is a good thing to be grateful. Positive thinking is having an optimistic view of the world as well as the future result of it. It's crucial to differentiate real optimism and "pink glasses" optimism and seemingly blindly looking at things as though they're going amazing. Realistic optimism is something all of us should aim for maintaining a healthy balance between believing that everything is going to be fantastic, while being aware that these things aren't going to happen by themselves and we'll need to work for that great outcomes. In the event that you manage to get the two combined, it's an excellent way to begin your day off with. The following affirmations could be helpful: "Today is a great day to work on my dreams and I'm going to do everything in my power to make them come true" and "I have a full body, a great mind and every step that I take is getting me closer to my goals" These are fantastic thoughts to begin your day.

3. Smile a lot

There's plenty of mental reasoning to force your self to smile. However, it's better to place yourself in circumstances that are certain to bring you joy, such as making a trip to the cashier and spotting that adorable woman you like or even watching some funny. People who are happy love to put themselves in situations that are smiling a lot. For example, if you are planning an event for your family so that you are able to visit your family more frequently, or going to visit your friend and make you smile can make your day more enjoyable.

4. Find friends with high-quality

It's best to have two or three top-quality friends rather than having 20 "drinking buddies". There's an abundance of people around the globe and you may not be able to connect with everyone. You're perfectly fine to be a party buddy and it's beneficial to have people you trust to be there for you should you require their help, regardless of whether you call at 3 a.m. whenever you need them. It's extremely important and beneficial to have the ability to view the people you like and consider, "Wow. This person is in my life for a reason, they add benefit to me, I love being around them. They're sticking with me for the rest of my life." If you are able to build a stronger network of relationships, ones lasting for a lifetime, with a solid, concrete foundation and will allow you to achieve a greater degree of happiness. Friends are characterized by a variety of psychological factors that can enable you to connect and be happy.

5. You've got to be a bad friend.

In your quest for a plethora of good friends most likely 80-90 percent of people you meet could be low-quality, harmful people that just want to profit from your situation, and it's time to eliminate them from your life. It can be a challenge to rid yourself of those who are like this, especially because they'd rather not appear as a pushy uncaring whenever they decide to cancel plans with a person. You can, however, avoid making plans so that you don't need to make a decision about cancelling. It is possible to avoid the person completely, and keep the least amount of contact with them as you can. It takes a lot of time to improve yourself and happier by removing the harmful people in your daily life.

6. You should take frequent breaks during your work hours

The study looked at using two types of individuals - one that didn't have breaks in any way in their (8) working hours, as opposed to the second group that took breaks of 10 minutes each hour. The results showed that the group who had breaks at least every hour did not have as much work time However, they felt happier, and more productive which meant they were able to get better work done than individuals who worked all 8 hours. Pauses allow your brain time to refuel and make you feel gratified (for breaks in themselves even if it's not to do some other reason) And you'll always get back to work with more enthusiasm to be more productive and work.

7. Create smart goals

Set goals that you can achieve which you'll be able to reach within a short timeframe can significantly increase the motivation of your. It's a lot of fun crossing that checkbox off of your list of things to do. When you set a goal, it is motivating, achieving the goal will bring a lot of pleasure and satisfaction. People who are happy set objectives that they will be able to reach and every time they achieve these goals, they gain increased motivation and discipline, and they achieve more with each new goal. The reward for success is always a positive factor for happiness.

8. Discover something completely new

If people who are happy become sad and depressed, they are forced to discover about something new. Whatever the case, providing your brain new ideas to ponder increases your creativity, and help you discover new pathways in your brain which will in turn assist the brain to be more healthy and help you become a happier person. When you're unhappy, depressed or are stuck feeling stuck The best ways to get out of it is learn things you've never heard of. The curiosity factor is a big help as it's boring to research topics which you don't like. Although it might not be appealing to you to begin learning how to play guitar, however you could be interested in piano, so start learning to play piano. Also, learn the best ways to care for your plants in a more effective manner. Find something that is fascinating for you and then learn the ways to take care of it. This will help you get past the tough times of your life. Take some time to relax and feed your mind with new facts.

9. Make sure you take care of yourself first.

If you've ever been on an airplane, you'll know that while they're going over the instruction and everyone is sitting, they do not mention, "In the case of an emergency, do not put your mask but try to help your children first." The way they phrase it is "Put your mask on first so that you can help the people around you." This is crucial to your personal development and, more specifically, in keeping your joy. It is essential to take proper care of yourself to ensure you're able to aid others. There's no way to assist others who are unhappy, depression is a factor, feeling down or you're broke financially.

10. Know the importance in helping other people

Contributing value to others' lives can bring you joy. Therefore, if you're finding that you're not effective in helping you overcome the depression, perhaps it's time to think about the qualities of others. Think about what you've got that will aid them to become more successful. The focus is taken off of you, and, instead of focusing on the inner turmoil of things going on in your mind and your life, you channel your mind's energy to consider how you can assist the other person in need This is more efficient, and can make you a more effective person for helping others.

Chapter 8: What You Can Do In Order To Live In A Healthier Way

Since it is vital to be healthy if you are to become healthy and satisfied The body is our most trusted partners so we must be sure to take care of them in the best way we can since your body is not the car you simply replace as it gets damaged. Your body will be there from beginning to end, and it's important to strive to look after it correctly. This is why we have 10 tips that will improve your health. If you implement them into your daily routine and you'll be healthier and possibly live for longer.

2.HAVE A FAVORITE SPORT

1. Get moving for at least 30 minutes every each day

Exercise can bring a myriad of benefits, ranging from psychological to physical. The heart pumps blood to the organs in a more efficient manner that are more oxygenated, you rid your body of toxins by sweating, your brain can be distracted from the stresses of everyday life while it also helps to refresh your mind and body. It's a good idea to exercise for 30 minutes. exercise is the minimum. And if the minimal amount is difficult create something you are happy engaging in. If you are a fan of lifting, do it, and if you love running, do it. If you are a fan of running, don't force you to lift. If you're not a fan of something take a chance to attempt to walk as much as you can. Make this decision using small items every day. You should ask yourself: "Do I really need to get my car from the bank, or am able to walk right to the bank? Should I actually drive the car to the store?" Or you can substitute the car for bicycle. In addition to being more healthy, but you'll reduce your impact on the planet and the environment as well.

2. Have you got a favourite sport

It's very similar to the previous one however, on a more extensive note. Personally, I'm not the biggest athlete, however, I enjoy having a game with my acquaintances, and it helps me get getting around for an hour each day. Actually, when I head out to play basketball with a group of friends I'm not even aware that the 30 minutes have been gone. The usual time is one or two hours then the sun was gone and I thought "Wow, I did not realize I spent that much physical activity enjoying the time with my friends."

3. Consume less calories

People who are healthy educate themselves on their food choices and the foods they consume on their body. This is something that many people are struggling over, since there's a myriad of misinformation and myths available on the web. However, the best thing can you do is decipher through the information. Read as many books as you can and begin to recognize and distinguish the myths from the reality. If you go to the nutritionist and study from those who've been studying for years about this subject. It's just a matter of continuing to be educated about your diet, the macronutrients and about calories. Everything from technical information to building muscle and losing weight this is crucial to maintaining your health. And lastly, be aware of your body! Be aware of how you feel following eating a meal. how energetic you are Are you feeling energized and fresh, or do you like to lay down and relax? What is it that you are craving? There are times that we yearn to eat junk food or salted snack foods, we are actually dehydrated, and our bodies want salt so they can conserve more the water. If you notice, sipping this glass of water could reduce your guilt too. Pay attention to the signals your body sends you, and with time you'll have an energised food plan.

4. Make a menu plan

It is essential to establish an organized schedule and ensure that certain food items don't contain any significant carcinogens. They will make you feel good and rejuvenated. People who are healthy eat specific vegetables more frequently as well as certain kinds of meals. Find out which combination works for you and stay away from eating excessive "junk food".

5. Sex (make lovers)

A few people may be annoyed by this. I'm talking about passionate intimate relationships with sexual partners that are not just a flirt or an occasional thing. There is no need to go out with a random person to have a sex session with them in order to improve your wellbeing (often often sleeping with strangers could cause you to develop unwanted illnesses instead of good health). Intimate, loving sex with a reliable partner releases far more beneficial and total chemicals in your brain than an occasional flirtation will. If you do are with someone, attempt to add some spice to your relationship, as sexual intimacy is an excellent relaxation tool, it pump your heart rate and energizes the entire body. If you do not have a significant other yet Do your best to build close, loving relationships, not just engaging in an evening of sex. It was my experience that in close relationship that lasts for a long time, those who are extremely healthy and who live for longer time and have had sex frequently.

6. At least two Liters of water each every day

It could seem like a amount of water to some people, particularly those who are typically having soda or pop all day long. Yet, simple water is the one your body truly demands. Other liquids, particularly tea, juices or coffee that contain other beverages, have additional sugars, calories and added sugar which you may not require. The water you drink can cause you to pee frequently this is a good thing since it helps keep your kidneys in good shape as well as helps rid itself of the toxins created in the course of a daily routine as a result of metabolism. Drinking plenty of water also improves your mood and helps keep your body in good shape.

Have you realized that the majority headaches that we suffer stem from dehydration, or something other than that? Most of the time, when you are taking a medicine to ease a headache it's not the medication which makes it disappear it's the water is consumed with it. Drinking two cups of fluids before you sleep will assist you in getting to sleep more comfortably and aid in waking up at the beginning of your day. Your bladder isn't equipped with the ability to snooze!

8. Enjoy time in the fresh air

There are a variety of opinions about this. It is believed which suggests that you need to get 2 to 8 hours of sunshine. Be aware that exposure to sunlight may cause skin cancers in the event that you do not protect yourself adequately from the risk. But, exposure to direct sunlight on the skin can help generate more vitamin D. Vitamin D is something is not available from any food source (vitamin D is crucial to fix calcium levels in teeth and bones). Some people also feel depressed when they're not getting enough sun and this is known as SAD or the Seasonal Affective Disorder. When you begin to feel down or depressed, a walk in the park or a book on a bench under bright sunlight could be just what you require.

8. At least 7 hours of restful sleep

There's a myriad of tricks that will help you get the best sleep. It is possible to sleep without the lights turned up, or even with strange sounds in the background however, it's not going to result in a high-quality sleep. Keep the light off, avoid drinking coffee for less than six hours prior to going to sleep Turn off all of the background noises, and turn the brightness of your mobile in the evening. It is not recommended to exercise or eating food for at least one hour prior to going to go to bed. It is possible to get your body for sleep for about 30 minutes and then perform a brief "ritual" before bed - turn off the lights, brush your teeth, get ready for bed and perhaps even read one or two pages in the book, or anything else that will help you relax and relax. An inviting and safe space is a signal to the body that everything is well and allows you to be a relaxing and peaceful place to rest. Why is sleep essential for well-being? This is because during the time that we sleep in the evening, all toxic substances that accumulate in our brain throughout the day (as the result of our metabolism and activities) are eliminated and the entire system cleanses itself and organs get an opportunity to perform through their "maintenance cycle" and repair any injuries that may be. To live for a long, healthy and happy life it is essential to get an adequate amount of sleep.

9. Do not forget to meditate frequently.

It is most well-known as a way to calm the mind and increasing happiness and peace of mind. Meditation also provides an opportunity for people to just be and be aware of your thoughts when they arise and how they move, and not try to control them. One mistake that people make when trying meditation first time is to make themselves empty their mind. It's actually the main aim of meditation but it's accomplished after a long period of practicing. A mind that is cluttered, and is able to have a million thoughts floating about, can be difficult to get rid of in a flash. Like a train, it needs to be reduced slowly. Therefore, at first, try to be aware of your thoughts and what they affect you. Consider your them as clouds in the ceiling of your head - clouds can appear and disappear but your attention should remain on the sky. There are numerous meditation strategies that are available, and I suggest you to experiment and determine which one works for your needs. The people who practice meditation for minimum 10 minutes a day can be found to be more focused, enjoy greater balance within their lives, and are less likely to experience a stroke just because they don't become annoyed as often.

10. Smile

Healthy people smile a lot. Smiles trigger the release of endorphines within the brain. This reduces stress since the act of using these muscles can lead to an optimistic mood and positive outlook. Additionally, smiling can be infectious it builds trust, therefore, if you smile when talking to anyone, they're more likely to aid to ease your burden. Additionally, it can also help make your work surroundings a little more comfortable and happy. There are numerous long-term positive health effects of smiling each throughout the day. Ensure that you're surrounded by positive friends, do hobbies you are passionate about and listen to music that will make your smile the most often you are able!

Chapter 9: What Are Bad Habits?

"I think if you stop bad habits, and you stop long enough, you develop good habits." Jordan Knight

An unproductive habit is the result of a negative behavior pattern. It's like an instinct that you have learned. If "your behavior" does not occur repeatedly, or occurs without conscious choice to perform it, then it's not really a habit. If you are doing the act without thinking about it, and that's why it's bad and calls for you to remove it.

The ability to acquire negative habits in a variety of ways. There is a chance that the undesirable behavior started in childhood which is why you've become familiar with it since you didn't have anyone to tell you what was wrong. Perhaps it's one you acquired because the influence of your peers; however, you could also find that you developed an undesirable habit as a result of trying to emulate a different person, for example actors or characters from a story. However you came to acquire your habit of bad behavior there is one thing that's certain about it: you need to get rid of it prior to it affecting the future of your development. The people are resentful of, mostly due to the fact that they are in violation of certain values that are significant including morals and practices. There are many people who have poor habits. Some, but not all with bad ones, consider them offensive or even annoying, (see the effect on relationships further below). In a certain degree, a negative habit for one person might not apply to the other person.

Imagine an epistemophilia with a brother who is known to spend a significant amount time time gaming on video. the epistemophilia would rather spend time looking through Wikipedia documents and solving problems and the other brother is obsessed with video games. Both are addicted to the things they like, but for certain people this type of activity or habit can cause problems in their lives, as well as deter the possibility of future success, such as cases of addicts to video games.

Everybody will admit that talking at a movie or in film screenings isn't a great idea because you're not sitting in your living area, therefore you'll just disturb people who are trying to focus on the film. If you are prone to picking your nose, or even rubbing your teeth while in public spaces, it is likely to deter others from your presence. Facebook is fantastic, but it is Netflix however, overdosing on these two resources or others is not a good idea! If you enjoy having high-heeled shoes all day, or using earphones for a long time, or eating a lot of red meat, be aware to protect your well-being! When you're not sure, or if you're procrastinating and avoiding distractions! There are a variety of naive habits that are harmful be detrimental to our efficiency levels. The list of harmful behaviors is inexhaustible! These are the habits are routinely performed every day with no time into it. These practices hinder your progress in life and can cause more harm than positive.

Are you in the habit of falling asleep early and getting up early? If you're aged or not it is time to end your habit right away! Human body requires adequate sleep and rejuvination to operate in a way that is optimal. If the human body does not have the adequate sleep required for the recovery of cells the possibility of premature death certainly be at the doorstep. Make sure you take care of yourself and don't let your routines over your life! The habits discussed above are fixable and how? It's by creating a healthy habit, of course. A established routine will often help. Making the routine is the most effective option. However, remember that the only method by which a person is able to change their bad habit is first acknowledging their habit. In the second, they must acknowledge that they has a problem with their habit. The denial process is very real and prevalent among all people and denying the bad habits which you carry every day and out, can restrict your ability to continue in the future.

Some other bad habits include taking a trip to the fast food restaurant for meals instead cutting fresh fruit and vegetables at home. chewing on your nails as working, eating and speaking with a mouth filled with food, and on. Are you employed in at a job that is not fulfilling you, and putting your tiny paycheck playing with your money for the rest of your life? Do you think that you'll be able to gain more money if you throw into a quarter more and one dollar? the bank account will grow into hundreds of dollars, then thousands? Then, you'll lose everything. If that's the case then you must recognize your issue, prior to cause a myriad of issues as a result of your poor habits that keep getting more and more difficult to overcome.

Acknowledging and acknowledging you've developed an issue or habit is the first step towards recovery. Continue to remind you that there's an issue that needs to be addressed and your habit of choice is actually, causing you to lose your lifestyle-- fast. When you accept that something needs to be changed then you'll begin to notice an internal transformation that will change your life to the positive. Remember that change inside can eventually translate into external change, which will make you feel better and more comfortable with your self as a whole. The body requires nutrition and structure. Remember this. There are times when we need to take a moment of silence in times of need, and sometimes we must take a examine the quality of our lives. This allows us the chance to improve our everyday life, well-being as well as the loved ones who surround us.

Chapter 10: Effects Of Bad Habits

The best method to get rid of undesirable habits is to replace the bad habits with positive ones. Jerome Hines

The negative effects of things happen Naturally, unhealthy habits cause harm that should be stressed! Negativity can affect everyone's lives from many and various aspects. It's important to be aware of the negative results your habits create and to understand the necessity of breaking these habitual patterns. Each of these effects will be discussed in further sections.

Prior to the book's discussion focusing on breaking bad behaviors that are the main objective of the book it's essential to remind readers that the number of harmful practices is a long one, which will the list of consequences can never be sufficient. The effects may vary from the ones that impact the quality of your life and your health (bad practices can leave you six feet below and in the grave) and the repercussions could cause you to lose opportunities, relationships and your chances of success for success in life. Habits that are harmful can alter the way you look and act and, as a result, destroy the relationships you have with people.

Health issues are among the most common and most severe results of unhealthy routines. It is important to prioritize health however, unfortunately, poor practices ensure that you put the health first. It is an unwise practice to place your health at the bottom of the list. If we aren't in good health in good shape, what are we to do succeed? If you're blessed by the health you deserve, then be happy and humble. As it is your greatest interest to develop healthy, positive lifestyles. Build your lifestyle around health in the near future, and you'll be able to see more happiness and success coming towards you. Poor habits could negatively affect individuals' health in numerous ways. Poor habits could lead to ailments, bad posture that lasts forever and even cause death, as previously mentioned.

For instance an individual who is who is addicted to social media activities like chat. The person spends a few hours staring at their smartphone screen and neck is placed at an uncomfortable angle. the habit eventually causes serious neck discomfort. Neck pain can cause anxiety, which results in the person who is achy getting into a battle with her or his spouse, due to the fact that they feel physically uneasy and annoyed, which can eventually ruin the relationships. Be aware that any bad habit can result in more negative behaviors. Someone who is used to biting their fingers could contract a bacterial infection through the process. The harmful bacteria and germs that are present in outside can quickly be introduced into our oral cavity during nail-biting. There is no doubt that nail-biting may affect the strength of teeth. The presence of bacteria and weak teeth is detrimental for our overall health. If you're someone who has this unhealthy behavior, in order to keep yourself from re-injuring your teeth take a moment to think about the effects of plaque and harm it can cause.

A third example, someone who is who has a habit of smoking cigarettes absolutely creates a risk uncertain health situation for their lungs. There's a rationale behind this statement: smoking causes premature death. This is the current general truth that smoking contributes to lung cancer. Unfortunately it is a disease that has no cure after it has gained the ability to hold on the organs of the host. One last instance is that of overeating. Anyone who is used to consuming excessive amounts of food can affect their health in numerous ways. The scientific evidence suggests that overeating causes your body to transmit incorrect signals to the brain. It makes you believe it is necessary to consume more when you've already eaten enough. Insulin resistance is a temporary result of excessive eating. Diabetes, obesity heart issues, and liver disease are the long-term consequences from eating too much. These are just a few examples to demonstrate how unhealthy practices can negatively impact your health. There is a chance that you are not a victim of all of the undesirable habits. If that's the case, then thus far, you're winning! It's important to determine the bad habits you have so that you can be sure to investigate the effects it has on your overall health. Keep in mind that this list of unhealthy practices isn't exhaustive!

The financial ruin of bad choices can be detrimental to your finances. Particularly in the case of a habit that demands a investment by the person you are. There is a tendency to pour cash into satiating your craving or desire to indulge in a negative behavior. When you combine every one of the little amounts you've paid for your bad behavior or a number of bad behaviors, the sum is enormous! It's even more devastating when the person who has the bad habit is restricted to financial matters. We'll consider someone who suffers from an addiction to gambling. In the beginning, his stake could be minimal or a small amount which isn't important. However, depending on how the game plays out, he/she might develop the desire to join an even bigger stake. Especially when the player is on an upward streak. However, after winning and wagers more and suffers at a sudden, huge loss. Someone who is addicted to gambling might bet on a piece that is valuable, for example the wristwatch of their telephone, or an old item of jewellery. This desperation will continue until the individual is at low. It continues to be so until the person is

buried in debt and at that point, the person usually recognizes that he has made a mistake. It is fine to indulge in a little bit every now and then. It may seem to be harmless initially however once it turns into an habit, it can be risky; keep in mind that the importance of moderation.

Food intake, as mentioned in the previous paragraph to show how poor eating habits could negatively impact your health, could be detrimental to your finances as well. It is possible to get the wrong signal regarding food intake when you're hungry. In this situation it is imperative to pay more for'stomach health', even when there is no need for additional food. Each extra portion of popcorn or ice cream in a sugar cone you purchase is just a penny additional or more of your budget. Take the small sums and find out how much you've splurged on things and items which do nothing to the consumer and can cause more harm than beneficial.

The smallest amount of money might seem small, but the accumulation of $2,000 put into the right way and with the benefits of compound interest could result in $234,781.71 over the course of 50 years. (this figure is calculated based on an average annual yield of about 10 per cent). Consider the long-lasting impact the new wealth may affect your retirement funds!

Costs associated with treating the health consequences of bad lifestyles is another method to impact your budget. There is health insurance. But remember that the health issue that you've incurred due to self-inflicted poor practices, could not be covered under your insurance policy. It might not be covered due to particular reasons. Perhaps you contributed to the health issues you've suffered. As an example, suppose you suffer from long-term respiratory problems which your physician determines the cause is smoking however, in your health insurance policy, smoking isn't considered to be covered. Similar situations occur frequently. At the end of the day, you'll be required to pay for it, just like being without insurance at all. Avoid going bankrupt due to inexperience about the health insurance plan you have and poor behavior. Begin by studying the tiny details and studying your future risk factors, prior to the negative consequences start to creep upon you some time later on. What you do now is likely to affect the future. The expense of fighting lung cancer that is caused by smoking cigarettes is a hard knowledge that should be absorbed by any person. Health costs associated with bad practices can be a major financial burden for anyone's long-term financial.

Opportunities can be destroyed: they could be hindered by our unhealthy behaviors. The first step is to think about the ways that undesirable habits impact your life Do you ever find yourself in a professional meeting and you are unconsciously chewing your nails when someone sitting beside you speaks to the audience? The audience members when they see these instances when you are chewing your nails tend to turn their attention to you instead of the person speaking next to you. Professionals present in the room might not be able to inform them with their mouths you're a tyrant and snarky, but they will tell you through the way they look at you. Because you're likely doing your nails with a conscious effort but you don't pick off the subtle signals which makes it appear that you're harming yourself by the results of your poor habits. People at the conference think you are unprofessional and conduct and carry the impression throughout the event in the near next. At the end of the day, employees won't have a positive impression of you, simply because of the bad habits that you have consciously implemented when you were in public. It's gross.

Imagine a scenario where someone has to decide between you and a different person and you require the manager or colleague of your profession to say a nice recommendation for you. Your mistakes and behaviors can deter them from your. Bad habits can result in harm either physically or professionally. It is a bad habit which can ruin your chances or your chances of success in world. It can end up costing you your job or take away the chance to win, and it happens every once. This is especially true that there aren't any deadlines to complete the job you're expected to complete. The idea of having a deadline assists the employee in coming up with an idea. If you have a deadline coming up that panic-inducing monster is usually awakened. Set deadlines, particularly in the event that you're having difficulty finalizing what you have started. They will give you an time period to plan your work which will give you plenty of time to establish your own daily goals. When you have achieved your goal set each day, a goal at one time and you'll soon be accomplishing more and more goals and will end up with a feeling of fulfillment in life as well as a sense of feeling completely satisfied.

Disrupting relationships: Some wrong choices could not be costly in terms of directly, but being late for work or even for an interview can. Poor habits can be costly as are on both sides. Bad habits could cost you your loved ones job. Unfortunate habits can destroy relationships or friendships. connection. Negative habits could cause your family to turn against you and turn strangers against them. Imagine a person who does not keep his word, and what said or done will be meaningless for people. He will be losing the trust of those around him as well as any trust they were able to have in his character. The girlfriend could be tempted to leave because of your actions and you could even push away your closest acquaintances in the end. Your spouse or mother might find it hard to challenge an accusation made against your character. The number of ways that bad habits could affect your relationship with other people is endless, and could affect not just your health, but to the people who are around you. Negative effects from bad habits could be harmful to people who are affected by the habits, based on the kind of habit they have. It can lead to death when they occur, for instance for women with bad diets; or having a diet that is too restrictive and not enough. It's been said many times, and our obsessions as well as our unhealthy habits have to be thrown out.

Be sure to educate you on the harmful practices and the consequences they cause. If one of your bad habits causes your life to be less normal Then you've resorted to bad habits. Do not fall prey to the bad habits you have developed beginning by recognizing your own shortcomings. The realization of this will propel your into the realm filled with good practices. We have to distinguish between healthy and bad practices. We should consider the risks and reward. If we want to compare good and poor practices, it is important to look at the future. If we look at the future, it is possible to determine what we can benefit from and what will not. the things that won't. Consider analyzing your present as well as your medium-, short-, and long-term objectives. Consider the steps you're taking in order towards achieving your objectives.

What is the place you would like to visit? Which place do you think you'll be most happy? Ask yourself in-depth questions in order to discover the underlying causes of your poor ways of living and the future you'll have and requirements. This type of question can help you identify ways to implement an inner change. Are you taking unneeded actions just by random chance? Do you have a way to be that is more effective?

Find ways to think outside the box and make a plan to make your life more enjoyable. The primary goal for cutting the bad habits we have is to minimize the quantity of stress our bodies experiences. Establish good habits that will ensure that your lifestyle is as easy as is possible. This can certainly bring about greater harmony in your daily life. Avoid causing yourself unneeded financial and emotional loss because of your poor behaviors. Your pattern is bound to repeat the same way as an old record. So make sure to end it now, whenever you are able! Do you recall when you were in elementary school that repeating the same pattern repeatedly, with the expectation of a different outcome is considered to be a sign of insanity? Avoid creating insanity within your own life. If you have inadequate control of your impulses and poor routines, get moving and then stop going backwards. Poor habits can cause a lot of negative consequences, such as laziness, financial and relationship losses as well as health concerns, time lost that you won't be able to recover, as well as bad consequences all the while healthy habits bring exactly the opposite.

Habits that are good for you can lead to goal-setting for a better life, financial and social stabilities, health and wellness habits that are preventative and time effectively spent. Being able to make a positive impact on life is about establishing healthy habits no matter the age at which you're. The goal of prioritizing your habits is to pile up the best habits in a way that you and all your efforts are successful. It is important to think about the future and consider the place you'd like to be in five or ten years. What about 20 years? These sorts of thinking needs to be always on the top of your mind so that you can take a risk-management approach to thinking. Knowing how to reduce the risk in your life reduces time and money, reduces the stress level, and gives us a peaceful state of feeling. Being calm can reduce your risk of suffering from heart disease or hypertension, and could even reduce your chance of suffering from an attack on your heart when you get older. Discover how you can fix the negative habits you have, through staying in the present moment and being fully cognizant and focused on today or tomorrow. And the future. Your future.

No one has a crystal ball for the future. However, making a plan, particularly in the event of a catastrophe, will aid in keeping us up to date. There will be challenges in periods of turmoil and uncertainty However, having a good habit will ensure that we are safe when we face the uncertain and unpredictable moments that are awaiting us in our everyday life.

Keep your reality under control Keep in mind that negative habits only create negative outcomes. Repeat this mantra to yourself whenever you need to.

Chapter 11: Breaking Bad Habits

But the issue is how can stop habitual behavior? According to Huffington Post, "new behavior is automatic, 66 days to be exact"1 This is true in certain people. The topic will be discussed in this subject more in chapter 4. To begin, you'll need be able to create the schedule you would like to incorporate into the new schedule or routine.

Begin with a daily schedule Then, plan your weekly tasks, and then your every month. As you progress to a level of professional the good habits you develop can be planned throughout the month. There are there are some novices taking this course, and should you be unfamiliar with good habit stacking and stacking, we recommend starting by jotting down your everyday routine. Every habit that costs your money or loss or turns out to be unhealthy, you should start removing it off the daily checklist that you're making. It will provide you with an idea of the things you are doing each day and it will tell the things you must quit doing.

This step can be taken up to the next step by writing next to the cross-out habit - your bad habit What is the reason for it to be bad? If, for instance, you smoke cigarettes, put it on the initial list since it's one of the things you do every day Then, you can take it off and then write down that it may lead to cancer. It is hoped that the "C" word can help you get to a more streamlined state for getting rid of your habit. This exercise for unwanted bad habits are present. This method is beneficial because it helps make your habit appear more visually concrete. Once the habit becomes tangible and visible, we are conscious of what we're unconsciously doing and can then employ anxiety as a strategy to break any bad habits we've developed. It is likely that fear will work in this situation.

There's a tendency for people to slip into certain patterns and vice versa, however if you inform yourself to not do it, and don't remain in the same place for too long -- If you begin being there for a long time it's likely that you'll fall into certain bad habits and I tried to not fall into that." Josh Duhamel

You've probably realized that bad behaviors are incredibly dangerous. It's like having cancer. should you be suffering from these habits, it is important to be quick to act before they spiral too far and destroy your life completely. Keep in mind that you were not naturally prone to these habits; you were exposed to them at one point in your life or the other. As they're not inherently and can be eliminated, it is possible to eliminate bad behaviors with just a bit or even a serious exertion. In the next section we'll provide further strategies that you can use in order to end the bad habits completely. Prior to proceeding, keep in mind that we mentioned at the start of the book that bad habits are diverse, and so while our focus will be broad. You'll have to identify your problem and tackle it using our strategies that we provide. In the event that specific examples are discussed within this book, just connect the overall concept to the problem you've found in you.

The decision to let go The first stage to break the habit. You must be motivated to stop the negative habit. It is essential to make a firm choice to break the routine and commit and devoted. It is essential to try all things to stop the cycle, but you have to be in this attitude to succeed. It is a matter of determination to end the bad habit. Keep in mind that the bad behavior can be a result of a conditioned impulse throughout your daily life. It is in your neural circuitry within the human body. Therefore, you require an enlightened mind and an unwavering determination to eliminate this bad habit out of your life! If the amount of determination isn't enough to keep you from getting back into the routine (mind that a failure to meet the requirements of the goal you had in mind does not mean you failed). Additionally, it's not enough to simply decide to give up; you must to be taught how to keep the habit.

A way to keep your willpower strong to overcome your bad habit is to keep it in mind, affirming yourself each day, that you're capable and worthy of it. Remember to do this every morning, or when you notice yourself reverting to your old habit - tell yourself you have to break the habit! It's not a problem speaking it to yourself. Another method to assist you in keep your resolve to end your habit is to practice positive thought. Never underestimate your ability to create transformation. Think positive and positively! Don't ever tell yourself that you cannot accomplish it. You may think it's impossible to change the bad habits you have however, that's thoughts of the opposing parliament that is saying! To overcome the inclinations of the negative thoughts that plague you it is important to remind yourself that you will succeed, and constantly think of those you have observed who succeeded in creating a lasting change.

Find and study your habit You must identify your bad habit you want to rid yourself of. Then, you can turn your drive for spontaneity into an eagerness to study. Curiousness killed the cat, not humans! Make sure you are curious about your behavior! The first step to conquer your foe is understanding the dangers you face! According to the old saying Keep your family close while keeping your enemies close. If you're in this situation, your habits that are bad for you can be your biggest adversaries. Look up additional books or resources to provide current and exact facts about the habits you're trying to break. Consider and consider the detrimental effects your habits could have on your life. If you recognize multiple bad habits, take care to focus on only just one problem one at one time. Be careful not to overwhelm your determination when you try to tackle multiple negative habits at the same time. There may be times when you need to put in the effort to rid yourself of several bad habits however, don't strain yourself out during this process, as it could weaken your resolve to eliminate one bad habit. Keep in mind that slow and steady is always the best way to win. Be sure to not tire yourself out prior to crossing the line of finish.

Develop a plan and eliminate triggers Once you have identified the negative behavior you must get rid of, the next important thing to do is to determine the triggers that cause the habit. If you are prone to the habit unconsciously or not, there's an event or something which make it happen. This could include the location, time, your mood and even certain things or people. Be aware of the need to end the habit to avoid the harm that it can bring, and set your mind to devise an approach to remove those triggers first, and then eliminate the behavior itself. Be aware that whatever plan that you come up with it is a must to adhere to the plan!

Let us provide some examples below. If you decide to get rid from gambling incessantly, lie in a comfortable position and attempt to determine the times, locations individuals, things, and places can be a sign of the presence of gambling. For instance, you could you will discover that it's usually that you are with certain people who make you gamble. It is possible that certain people come to bring you home, and then you take a trip out. You may also find that you're betting at night after working, and taking the same route back home. Could the trigger may be an online or mobile app? Do a thorough task and note these triggers in your notebook each time you want to bet.

Sure, it sounds as if you're working too hard, however, don't forget the adverse effects that gambling can have on your daily life. Absolutely, don't ignore the pricey jewelry or home you borrowed and then lost! Find out the problem, and then solve the issue. If not, nobody else can help you. When you have identified the factors, you can eliminate them entirely or alter your relationship with these people. It is possible to limit the amount of occasions you spend with your buddies by giving legitimate excuses, like assigning yourself tasks to finish within a certain duration of time, and also the time you're expected to be spending with your friends. You can also tell your gambling acquaintances that you spend time hiking rather than gambling the next day or tomorrow. Create an excuse real repeatedly. Then you will realize that you're replacing your bad behaviors with better ones. You should begin this process as soon as you notice the signs of bad habits appearing.

Select a companion or handler The idea is to allow someone to be in about your plans and objectives as well as having them support you keep it on track. They must be someone who you trust, or trust, as well as who you are able to trust and not be disappointed, like your partner, mother as well as your closest friend. your mentor. Let them know what is going on and what you're doing to fix the situation. Make them read the book to know how to implement your plan and not criticize your failures.

Maybe the person you select as your trusted friend may be attempting to stop their addiction If this is the situation, then be there for you, and they'll help you as well. Take a look back at our previous example of gambling. If a friend is the one who triggers your gambling addiction it is possible to have an honest conversation with them about it and let them know the desire to end your gambling. If they're interested and want to join in, then every one of you will be an ally to one another when it comes to breaking this habit.

You and your friend could go through this book, find out about the specific habit and its consequences, create strategies, and make sure you follow up on your weekly check-ups and offer support should either of you failing to meet the criteria of the goals. If your friend is unwilling to take you seriously, we recommend that it could be time to stay clear of this particular person, since they may not be thinking of your best interests at heart.

Create Rewards and Challenges A great strategy to stopping a habit adding challenges to your program or process. It is possible to set a goal as well as a target for yourself Then, you'll be able to attempt to overcome the obstacle and reach the desired goal. The goal and challenge have to be time limited. This is the only way that it can work. In order to be more effective it is essential to start out with short periods of time before moving on towards longer intervals of time. In the case of, say, you're planning to end drinking, incorporate in your strategy not to drink alcohol for three days in a row. At the end of those three days, you may enjoy a drink. Say glasses. Then, you can continue your commitment for another 3 days, after that, seven days, 2 weeks, one month and after that, for six months. Add more tasks and days to your plan Sooner or the time, you will not want to drink any more. Your body won't just become healthier, but also your brain.

When you finish every time-bound challenge you can choose to reward yourself with different than alcohol (we recommend that you find out more about your personality and what you love in order to determine the right reward for you). Alcohol is a good reward after the three initial tasks, however it should be small quantities, take a sip or two and no less. This will prevent the relapse back into your drinking habit, which you have been avoiding for years. It is essential to eliminate your craving for a period of time before rewarding yourself only with a small amount after the time of starvation. It is important to have a great deal of determination not to indulge whenever you offer yourself a reward. You must constantly keep reminding yourself that you will achieve it!

The challenge may take the form of your routine. Keep in mind that even small victories and achievements are also important. If you are drinking the equivalent of five drinks every each day. Make it your mission to spend for a whole week drinking 3 bottles of alcohol per day. In the following week the amount can be cut down to just two bottles per day and the following two weeks, you can drink one bottle per day. When you've finished the first month, you may alter your goal to a great extent: it is possible to limit your consumption to 2 bottles per month for the duration of a month. such as one on Fridays, and one on Saturdays. This reduction will continue to be as such until you're reduced to one bottle per week, a bottle every month, or one bottle after 6 months.

In the case of drinking and addiction to drugs The human body typically becomes physically dependent on this bad habit. This is the reason it's essential to slowly ease your body from alcohol or drug. If you've been drinking or taking drug use for too long and then suddenly cut off the substance or alcohol and your body goes into shock, and severe physical effects could occur. If you're struggling to breaking a habit of drinking or a drug addiction, it's recommended to speak with a qualified professional prior to making any decisions, as to ensure that you're in safe in the hands of a professional. If you're not seeking professional assistance, gradually weaning your way off can also work and it requires total commitment and an unwavering determination.

Assess Your Progress: After you've established targets and objectives for yourself, it is important to assist yourself in achieving the objectives. One way for you to achieve this is to track the progress you have made. It is possible to dedicate a journal to your plan or allow it to be easily tracked making use of a mobile app or computer program including a spreadsheet to keep your record. Draw illustrations of your strategy and the progress you have made. The method you have chosen to break the bad habit must be discussed with the individual you've chosen. As you do not wish to be a disappointment and you might be tempted to lie about your progress in order in order to impress them. If you make changes to your noted performance, you're not helping you, in actual it is a waste of your time and time. Make sure you are honest with your data Your records show you where needs to be improved on; the notes you make will show whether or not you're slipping or are improving.

A different method to gauge the progress you have made is to keep the track of how much the loss would be should you have continued with your old routine. Consider a scenario where you shift between drinking 5 bottles every day to just three. Certain, the amount that you pay for it will decrease. Make it your intention to reduce a certain quantity of time or money from your habits that are harmful over a specific time period, You can then determine the amount (time or cash) you've saved at the end of your time. You can compare the current amount to what you'd lost earlier on due to the wrong behavior. You can then purchase some memorabilia, or even more valuable items using the savings for a lasting reminder of your success.

Stopping Cold Turkey: One mistake that many people who are trying to break an unhealthy habit commit is not quitting cold turkey i.e. the act of stopping immediately or abruptly. It is because they are aware of the harm the habit resulted in for their lives. This method can work, especially if you can prove that the repetitive nature of the problem is not too severe as a result of different motives, such as viewing that the behavior as a crime according to a religious viewpoint. In reality, the approach is not enough, those who are trying to get rid of a negative habit is likely to return to the same habit.

The bad habits should be removed gradual and not suddenly as this is the sole option to make sure that the desire or urge is gone from your brain. If you follow a slow and constant pace, it's likely that someone will occasionally slip, or slip back into their old behavior, but this is a normal occurrence. It isn't considered to be an attempt to fail in any way. Actually, it just indicates that the individual isn't stopping abruptly. Give yourself the space to slip up or a missed opportunity. All of us are humans and nobody is flawless! Most important is not to let slips off, falling or tripping to hinder us from getting to the other side of the fence and reaching our goals. You can simply pick yourself up, and resume the journey in the same direction you started. When you're back up make sure you don't let down the person you are working with or let your partner to beat your performance. You should have a partner who can help you stay in a stable position and vice versa.

Connect a Loss to or Reward Youself: linking losses to the fact that you fall from the goals will also assist you in sticking to the program. Nobody likes losing. In an unhealthy habit-breaking process together, think of this as a game that you cannot be a part of. Make it clear that the process must be an win-win situation for both of you as well as you. If you are finding yourself doing your efforts on your own it is possible to include into your strategy every time you violated your plan and donate one dollar towards charity or another worthwhile reason. You will be liable for each time you violate your plan guidelines.

In the opposite way, you could give a prize to your accomplishments. It is important to be rewarded for the work you've done and not just when the job is done, but all through you are working. There is a supervisorSomeone who is grateful for your effort and inspires you to be better. You can reward yourself with a few things every time you reach a target within your strategy. At the end of the day, when you've successfully got rid off the path of addiction then give yourself a greater reward, or have your supervisor promise to help you achieve that goal.

When you have written your plan, ensure that you put your rules of best practices at a location where you will see it every day. This is the time when you must adhere to the plan. At first, it may be difficult because it's not your normal routine of following the plan you've made for yourself. However, whenever you're willing, there is always the way. You will have to constantly hear the phrase. Follow through with your plan and routine As time is passed and the new routine is likely to be second nature and will eventually become a part of your routine, just like to the old habit as well as the way you carried it out.

Chapter 12: 66 Days Before A Habit Becomes Automatic

The average time is 66 days begin a new routine. Many may believe that the number that is magic is 21 as it is a legend has been circulated, since a plastic surgeon, Dr. Maxwell Maltz, noticed an increase in his patients back in the 1950's. The Huffington Post reports, the surgeon performed nose surgery which took the patients 21 days to adjust the new face.2 Like a patient who had an amputation and amputation, the patient took about 21 days to adjust to the new appearance. In this instance the '21-day myth of habit is not true, since the instances mentioned aren't habits and are definitely in the realm of physical recovery.

If you help a positive habit, it will become automatic. it requires time. If you've reached the 66-day milestone and you've reached the climax stage. Keep in mind that the days that lead up to this achievement will be difficult. If you don't get it done and you could be tempted to return to old ways and methods, as at first this is a simple thing to accomplish.

It is easy to overlook our goals for the future; for example, you could think of building wealth to be a good neighbor and by donating money to research since you have lost family members in the battle against cancer. It's crucial to discuss the goals we have with us each day when we get up. Talk about your goals with your mentors. We strongly recommend sharing your goals in order to turn them into an actual reality. Then, develop plans to reach your targets. Make a note of the main objectives and goals on post-it notepads and put it in front of the mirror each morning. As you are brushing your teeth contemplate one way you'll do for yourself to achieve your goal that you can see in the mirror.

The long-term objectives you have set for yourself must look as clear and as bright as blue sky because your constantly changing. It's not beneficial for you to alter your behavior for someone else except you. If you're making the change to help someone else, the chances that change is going to be temporary. Most of us return back to our old ways when time goes on towards the future. In earlier chapters, if you take your time as you progress to creating a habit that is automatic within about 66 days. When you have done this then you're in the right direction towards complete elimination of bad habits and future ease.

2 https://www.huffingtonpost.com/james-clear/forming-new-habits_b_5104807.html

Chapter 13: Kiss Bad Habits Goodbye Forever

After you've learned several strategies to implement positive habits in your daily life You can now learn to put down bad habits for good. The best way to go is to create an excuse to stop your negative behavior. The aversion is likely to result in an aversion to your thoughts and actions of the habit the goal is to get rid of.

To prevent aversions, it is necessary to study and gather a lot of information regarding the effects of the bad habits you have. When you confront yourself with the awful truth behind your habit it will be difficult to repeat it. The importance of knowing is power. The more you are aware of consequences of your poor habits and the more likely it is that you'll continue carrying your bad habits along with you.

For instance, suppose you're consumed by eating a lot of high in sugar and aren't able to stop, regardless of the effort you put in? Every time you have a craving to eat, you fill your stomach with the most sugar-rich food you can imagine. Don't do it! You've recognized the bad routine. Your bad habit is your inclination to eat sugary foods when you get a spare period. Use this time when you normally choose sugar or chocolate and begin reading about the negative health consequences from eating too much sugar. Since the internet is easily accessible to everybody these days, information can be found on almost every topic.

Just go to Google and begin reading the first article that comes up. Continue reading. Try this daily, or any time you are feeling desire to go from food items that are sugary to sweet. What are you discovering while doing your research? We are sure that you learned that eating excess sugar while young may lead to the development of many diseases long-term. What kind of diseases do sugary foods trigger? Diabetes, cancer, it could lower your body's immune system and so on. If the diseases you are suffering from don't stop you from getting them continue reading, and make sure you check the news for research and medical advances.

We all know that medical information is changing every day as there is constant research that's conducted. You are prone to touching your nose, eyes, or mouth with your filthy hands. There is a possibility that you always get colds. You may do this as a nervous habit--subconsciously. It is likely that others will are aware of this habit and you are not saying any words. Be aware in the present moment, and begin to be aware of what you're doing prior to engaging in the act.

It's never a bad decision to establish the habit of regularly washing your hands. This is especially important when you eat. Do this each time you cough or wheeze. This is especially true while you are using the bathroom or work with animals or dispose of garbage.

It is essential to remain conscious of what you do. You must learn the essential health practices so that the body's immune system will be healthy. Flu season is getting worse each year, as it replicates, and is able to fool doctors each year. Influenza viruses can infect the people around them through tiny drops of blood that circulate floating around. Make it the habit of not going out when you're sick and make sure you get your vaccine for flu! Implementing these health-related habits can ensure that you live longer and healthier. Who ever said being healthy and alert is a bad practice?

Chapter 14: In With The New, Out With The Old

If we are thinking about something new and fresh, we definitely don't like to contemplate the old ways of doing things, definitely not! This article is to be for all of us. The old ways have to be completed, particularly in order to progress towards a better and more efficient kind of life. This isn't easy. Be attentive and study. When you've finally said the bad habits you have cultivated You must begin informing your brain to stop thinking about your old habits. There are some who do not be able to get rid of the old ways of doing things. It's not difficult to slip back into your old habits routine.

Examples: You are aware that If you are tempted to relapse back into drinking or sugar or don't wash your hands' practice, the result could be death before it's time. Are we really going to want to die young and feel happy? Feel good about yourself through activities that soothe your spirit. Let go of the past and start incorporating new routines. If you love to garden or workout and cook, walk, or ride a bike, go out and enjoy it! Do not wait until tomorrow. In time, you'll start to see that good habits can will make you feel more comfortable than the bad habits you opted to eliminate.

Who doesn't like being overweight from all the sugary drinks? Who likes the feeling of discomfort in the liver or kidneys due to the blurred nights of drunken drinking? Or, worse yet, does anyone want worrying about being sick all the time? It is possible to protect yourself. to be in the present and to leave the previous. The first step to establishing good habits is being healthy, therefore consider your longevity in the future. Healthy living and being healthy is the ultimate goal of everyone. Get started by creating a health strategy for your life; however, you must tailor your plan to suit you. Recognizing your habits and conducting your own research is a good start towards a healthier lifestyle and especially because you've made it this far and have decided to change your ways and live a healthier living by studying this book.

If you study the negative ways you behaved every day You will observe that your bad habits could cause problems in the future. Everything we consume in our bodies on an ongoing basis eventually starts to be manifested into our bodies and we must be fully aware when it comes to the things you put into your body, the one that was given to you. It is true that history has a tendency to repeat itself which is why it's imperative to learn from the mistakes that others have made. This is the reason we stress the importance of learning about the negative behaviors. For instance the character Charlie Sheen, is known to be totally in control. He had an extravagant Hollywood life, consuming women and men, as well as in alcohol, drugs, you know what. These bad habits of lifestyle finally caught up to his health, and today the actor. Sheen has to live the life of an illness that lasts for a lifetime, HIV. If he'd been a bit more cautious and more introspective and logical, he would have been able to avoid this devastation for the rest of his life.

Take Amy Winehouse's insidious ways and take lessons from them. She has a great voice however, Hollywood was devouring her the moment she got known. The poor artist began taking drugs in large quantities and ultimately ended her life because of the addiction to heroin. Making mistakes and learning from them that other people make in their lives is certainly a traumatic experience, but such instances could help us learn from our children a lesson.

The key is not to repeat the same old behaviors because we do not wish to suffer the negative consequences which come from the bad habits that we've cultivated. Be aware of your own actions, or you'll end up frozen in the frigid cold and no one willing to assist you other than yourself. Stand strong and stay long.

Chapter 15: Leave The Old, In The Cold

No one likes being cold. Of course it is true that there are some who love winter sports and are awed by the frigid temperatures. However, let's say this again nobody likes cold and snow. Start by putting our habits to the ice. Then, smash the ice using an enormous stick! Take a look at your past bad habits broken into small pieces you are able to sweep get rid of from your living. There's no reason for us for us to go back to the old routines.

As we progress and begin to adopt new routines, we should continue to follow these habits. It was possible to teach our minds to avoid repulsions towards our bad habits from the past by using research-based methods to guide us off from the past poor practices. Maybe we were riding the fast foods every day following working because we were tired. If this is your situation, then we strongly suggest that you stay off from this habit to begin a new, more healthy lifestyle. Studies have shown that eating the consumption of unhealthy food could cause serious health issues in the future or even deadly! The mere fact of death could create fear in anyone who is susceptible to changes. Learn as much that you can lay you hands on. Be afraid of your previous poor behavior. It is an effective tool to keep yourself from bad habits.

The strategy has proved to work and effective, but has proved to be a lot of resemblance because the moment you're scared of something, it is easier to be cautious about it This is why. For instance, if you're a gambler but find it hard to maintain your weekly check into your bank account since you are addicted to gambling. you don't set goals for yourself. So instead, you burn up your cash, and you even resort to credit cards, in order in order to help you with your dangerous addiction. So, you're done!

One of the things you must do is join an Gamblers Anonymous assistance group, where you'll be taught real strategies regarding how you can stop from gambling. It's not just an unhealthy habit, it is it is a dangerous addiction that could be a threat to your health and caused a lot of harm to people's lives. The best thing to do is sit down and stop thinking about the blinking lights and the high-pitched sounds and consider ways to ensure that your cash is safe and on your bank account. It is time to begin studying 'bad habits of gambling to understand that it's not just only about amount of money. The reason for your addiction lies in being numb to the daily life experience when you're actually seeking a way to escape by gambling. It is a method to manage the issues you face but the longer-term result may not be so great because the shady behavior can leave you broke or homeless and even broke.

Don't ruin your life by committing to a negative habit or addiction. Find a way to replace your destructive habits with positive ones in the near future, and you'll notice that your health and life has improved rather than declining.

We'll give you another scenario, maybe you're lazy and it's difficult for you to get out of your bed earlier, so you opt to get up and start working from 12 to nine. It's okay but at least you're doing your best, but working hours that are beneficial to aren't always working for someone else who is working right next to you. Consider the situation this way: suppose you're trying to make more money, and have your own company, If this is the situation then a 12-to- nine time slot isn't optimal due to the simple nature of businesses generally starting working earlier. It is the norm in this world. Not every large business is a vampire. Shape to get dressed and go out.

There is a myriad of undesirable habits that are difficult to be able to break. The process of breaking bad habits requires determination, strength determination, constancy, and strength. The power is in us to control our minds as well as our bodies. Don't let your thoughts and your body take control of your life. The book's goal is to assist you in thinking outside of your head, and out of the circle you've created, and is designed provide a range of options to assist you make a significant improvement. You can get out of that low-key slump, lift your head up, and begin the process over in the event that you must.

Every day is a brand new day that allows us to begin fresh. There are always bad times and bad habits however, knowing what we can do to be the most effective version of ourselves is crucial to the future success of our lives. Set out to end the stress and negative habits with a brand new routine. If you use tobacco and you find it difficult to stop because of your physical dependence and we are aware you must take each day at an time. It is important to have additional support and assistance; it is impossible to completely quit our addictions on our own and that is the reason why we recommend that consult your physician for permission to provide the patient with a patch. The goal is to gradually ease your way off from smoking.

Chapter 16: Planning Your Routine 10 Proven Strategies

Learn to strategize and prepare your schedule before you set out to conquer the world. Your destiny is in your hands We are just one We are definitely not perfect. However, be aware that practicing will result in perfection, but one day.

1. PLAN YOUR DAY

If you can plan your work day around the schedule you have set and adhere to your plan, you'll be able to see the efficiency you desire with ease. Effectiveness will help you have more efficient workdays, greater tasks accomplished equals greater achievements. Begin by thinking about your work schedule. What time is the time you must start work? If you're working for yourself what is the ideal time to establish working time? Like we said earlier If you're working as a sole proprietor, be sure to make yourself accessible during business hours that are normal in order to increase the quantity of businesses that you join. Business-to-business marketing is crucial, as when you are unable to effectively market to other companies what do you earn money? Do not start the day too late Start your healthy routines earlier.

It is a fact that money doesn't purchase happiness. It provides comfort. The more well-organized and precise your life is, the greater comfort you will be able to provide yourself, however be aware that health must come first. When you have figured out your plan you must follow, ensure you record it, or write it down. Then, you can break your work day into time blocks. This way you will be able to learn how to the stack.

2. START A ROUTINE

Now that you have a schedule you can adhere to, and the morning routine through your evening routine can be planned completely. After you have completed this step, you've got an important foundation to build from. Make sure you follow the rules set by your organization, since it's obvious that the rules you follow have long-term objectives as well as a scientifically-proven research that supports your plan routine. It is going to be a win-win situation.

3. TAKE ULTIMATE CARE OF YOURSELF

If you are not in fitness level in good shape, your abilities will be limited with regards to routine tasks. It is crucial to maintain a healthy balance between your body, mind and your body. Consider adding more fluid into your daily diet and getting rid of processed and saturated food. Begin by eating meals that are organic as well as avoiding animal products that contain antibiotics and pesticides as the chemicals and medicines are proven to be detrimental to humans over a lengthy time. Check the labels on your food and don't trust any firm that sells their product in the marketplace. Make sure you are skeptical. The brain and our bodies require specific nutrients in order to reach their optimal capacity, therefore make sure you change the way you live and taking healthy food choices like complete grains, lean cuts of meat as well as more fluid water. fresh washed vegetables and fruits that don't contain any harmful chemical substances.

4. MODERATION IS KEY

Avoid having too much alcohol at the dinner table while trying to get rid of your unhealthy habit Drinking will restrict your capabilities and cause you to slip off your productive habit. The alcohol will make you get lazy and then relapse back into the same bad habits over and over again.

If you are drinking be sure to maintain the limits to a minimum because external substances are acknowledged to change brain's circuits. Alcohol and drugs do not benefit people who engage in an exercise. Keep everything you are doing in moderate your consumption. Your body will be grateful for this when you get getting older.

5. HOBBIES

Instead of engaging in the bad habits you have ensure that you find activities that will replace your poor practices. If, for instance, you're habitually sitting for hours in your job Maybe request your boss to buy an adjustable desk This way, you will be able to get rid of the habit of sitting all day long.

The people who are sedentary can also be prone to issues with health in the future because our bodies are designed to move.

Be sure to keep this phrase at hand A body that is in motion is always moving. It is possible to replace your sitting routine with a regular nighttime exercise on the treadmill. it will make you healthier both in and out. Begin with an inch, after that, run for a mile. it's that easy. Do not go too far because too much work out can lead to a exercise habit. In terms of your passions, as you aren't creating any problems with your personal life, you're on the right track.

6. COMMUNICATION IS KEY

Anyone who has bad habits must be honest about the bad habits they have with their partner in crime as well as family and friends This is extremely crucial. Naturally, they will know about your negative habits prior to you, however it's crucial to engage them in a conversation and tell them that you are aware of your poor behavior. Make them aware that you're taking a deliberate effort and determination to improve. This may save your partnership/relationships if your bad habits seem to affect your significant other, or your family and friends. Keep it up and be sure that you must always honor your commitments. In the event that you fail to do this, other people might not believe you. Remember the kid who had a nightmare numerous times. No one believed in his story, until he violated the promise he made to himself.

7. MEDITATE

There are times when we're anxious and overwhelmed It is not difficult to become overwhelmed. You need to get rid of this pattern and figure out how to manage our stress by focusing on the external. You might think of taking a yoga classes to reconnect with your self? Yoga can be a great routine that helps ease the stress of life and also assist you in becoming more aware of the rhythm of your breathing, as well as the simple things in your life. Take time to relax as it will assist you with planning the next step in your the world.

8. EXPLORE/ADVENTURE

You must ensure that you give you sufficient time off, get out and discover the beauty of nature. Human bodies love to go outside, and it needs Vitamin D for survival and to keep it well. Be sure to exercise regularly throughout the course of your week. If we aren't exercising and our minds become hazy and this can lead to low concentration. Going outside may provide a sense of calm and refreshment. Make sure you go outside to explore and then protect your body with sunscreen during the course. A break from your normal routine is a necessity at least once in a while. It's true that the purpose behind getting rid of bad habits is in the form of habit-stacking and that is why it's good to go on a journey whenever you have the chance. Naturally, you should think about your trip and contemplate the places you'll go to and the amount it is going to cost prior to jumping onto the next flight. If we think about vacations, it helps us relax, and it feels as if we've got a plan in the back of our minds.

9. GIVE MEANING

Find meaning in your life. Consider your life as an experience. You are alive, and you discover every day. Explore the world and start giving back to the universe that has provided the best living. The world is filled with abundant things; it is important to make your life meaningful through a deeper understanding of your self and figuring out what you're meant to do. If you select the profession you're made to pursue, you'll give an opportunity to others. Say, for example, you're a genius in the field of technology. Then it is best to be in the field of science and technology which will allow you to assist people advance in forward action. Do something for the world by doing your best at what you do. Everyone needs a bit of aid in finding the talents are honed in our inner. We suggest to be to eliminate all your ideas. In the next step, get your head clear, it is time to consider what you are most happy about? What do you excel at? What brings you joy? The answers to these questions could provide a solution which will help you determine what causes you to be satisfied. Find something that you can see your self doing continuously This way, you will never lose interest in your job--which is your goal. Make sure you have a good relationship and keep them healthy. Being in a good relationship helps to keep us on track with our routines, which include healthy routines. Spend time to take a moment and do something kind to someone regardless of how large or insignificant it might be. Keep your heart humble, friendly and thankful. These traits aid a person to become more focused on their goals. We have learned that keeping your word is essential regardless of the situation, whether it's private or business; if you don't have the commitment to keep your word, you likely don't have anything in the first place.

10. PRACTICE MAKES PERFECT-- PERSEVERE

We've all learned that over time there is no way that a human being can be perfect We must make sure that should we get back to our previous negative habits, we have be able to find a way to get ourselves up from the hole of rabbits. Don't forget to look up the specific habits that you are guilty of by typing in Google"fast food craving,' gambling addiction', 'not cleaning your hands or removing germs from the kitchen,' you'll find many reasons to cause you to want to stay away from any negative habit you have. Poor habits do not bring anything positive in the long run. They only cause us more challenges The cons are evidently greater than those benefits. If you're interested in making changes, it's not too late. Accept that you're not perfectly. If you've developed your smoking habit and then quit smoking and be aware that you're inflicting harm on your lungs, and are exposing yourself to chronic health issues, which can hurt physically. Everyone hates getting in a state of sickness, therefore it's on us as the person, to adopt an habit of extending our life span. Being proactive about our health could lead to greater progress throughout the world as we understand it. The more we understand about ourselves, the more stronger. All of it starts with you, the person who is at the center. Learn to build healthy routines. If you smoke, substitute your habit with exercise instead it will help your cilia recover (tiny hairs which push foreign and harmful substances from of your lung). If you smoke, cilia needed for protection against illness are affected, and often damaged, making the lungs vulnerable to developing illnesses. Take the first step to give your lungs a rest Take it slowly all day long and every day out. In the event that you do not, your physical withdrawal will be a major issue. It is a constant reminder the need to change your habits of the past with new and healthy habits for just the fact that repetition builds habit, which is good practices, as in this case.

www.ingramcontent.com/pod-product-compliance
Lightning Source LLC
Chambersburg PA
CBHW051725020426
42333CB00014B/1155